ACKNOWLEDGMENTS

I would like to say a heart-felt thanks to my family for their continued patience during the time I was involved in studying and writing this book. There were many days that I was found in deep study when I was needed by them. I appreciate their love and understanding. I especially thank my wife for her encouragement over the years. Thank you, Corkie, my best friend.

I thank Pleasant View Baptist Church, in Port Deposit, Maryland, for the inspiration to continue in labor for Christ. I thank all the members for their inspiration and encouragement. I would also say a hardy thanks to Bear Spring Baptist Church of Dover, Tennessee; Sylvia Baptist Church of Dickson, Tennessee; Eunity Baptist Church of Cheraw, South Carolina; Trace Creek Baptist Church of Mayfield, Kentucky; Flat Rock Baptist Church of Starr, South Carolina; and Friendship Baptist Church of Honea Path, South Carolina, for their love, patience and investment in my Christian growth.

I also would like to thank my parents, Billy Ray and Annie Ruth Phillips, my brothers Brian, Steve and David Phillips, and my sister Cathy Kennedy, for their encouragement these past years. Thanks so much for being there.

I also give a word of thanks to those who have labored before me to bring this evidence to light. Others have laid the foundation upon which I am building. Thank you.

Thanks also to Bart Thomas and Gayle Leubecker for their labor as we brought this book together, as well as the other staff in the office at Pleasant View: Amanda Humphreys, Lauree Wilson, Lora Moody, Melissa Kozminski and Pastor Chris Engelberth. Thank You.

Scripture quotations are from the King James Version of the Bible.

TABLE OF CONTENTS

    Introduction
1. Understanding why people do what they do
2. Understanding how I came to this truth
3. Understanding the word "love"
4. Pictures of love levels in the Bible
5. Explaining the five levels of love
6. Why "apple eating" in Genesis is called "the fall"
7. Discussing why people do what they do in light of the five levels
8. How to discover your love level
9. Moving from level one to level five
10. Understanding how moving from one level to another affects our lives
11. Understanding how our love level affects the decisions we make from one day to the next
12. Understanding why progressing through levels is essential to serving God effectively
13. Mastering level five love is our ultimate goal
14. Biblical examples in light of five-level understanding
15. Understanding the need to move to level five (agape) and how to stay at level five

16. With what we know now, let's examine a few issues
17. A personal note
18. Conclusion
19. A bonus, but a must

INTRODUCTION

What is the most powerful force in heaven and earth?

Why do people do the things they do?

How can the answer to these two questions help us understand people as we do what we do, and make the choices we make?

Every part of life and death is affected by this source of power. Even one of God's top three angels struggled with this issue, and was affected by this power. We understand that God created a host of angels, and one of the chief angels came to a time when he would turn against his own Creator. From studying many passages in the Bible, we have learned that the devil we know of today was once an angel of God in heaven. He became filled with envy towards God and wanted to be like God. He led a revolt of angels in heaven, and God made him (and those who followed him) leave heaven. When we finish this study, I believe you will see that even the devil is caught up in the love level choice.

I also believe when we finish this material, we will understand what is the most powerful force in our universe. Every power source is fueled by something, and people are no different. When man discovered the power that comes from splitting the atom, atomic energy was the result. It was there all the time, but until someone discovered the source of power that is harnessed when the atom is split, the power was hidden. Atomic energy is both a powerful blessing and a powerful curse. So is the power of love. I believe that when you grasp what I have discovered, you will understand that the level, the direction, the procession of love will govern your abilities in life. This information is a must for every person that wants to succeed in life!

It is a wonderful thing when God allows us to discover truths that consistently take place all around us. I am penning this information so that the truth that I have been privileged to discover can become part of your world also. This insight answers so many of my questions about people: how they think, whom they are committed to and why they do things. One person will give their life to save another's in a life-or-death situation, but a second person, when put into the same situation, may not be willing to sacrifice anything. Why is it different? I contend that it is not just love but *levels* of love. When you read and comprehend this discovery, you will understand so much about why people do what they do.

Several years ago, a wonderful discovery was made by Dr. Gary Chapman, a pastor and counselor in North Carolina. Dr. Chapman discovered that God designed five ways to communicate love. When he saw this in

God's word as well as God's creation, he said that it changed his life. Let me say that it changed mine and millions of others' lives as well. If you haven't read the book by Dr. Gary Chapman "The Five Love Languages," you must read it -- it will change all of your relationships. I am glad that Dr. Chapman did not keep the love language material to himself. Millions of people have been changed by their understanding of how love languages work.

This material has the potential of doing the same thing as we love God and love others. All of our relationships are governed by our love relationships, and this discovery in God's design is a must for anyone who wants to know how to change their life and the lives of those around them. You must read Dr. Chapman's book, and you must read on as we uncover these rich elements of transformation.

CHAPTER ONE

UNDERSTANDING WHY PEOPLE DO WHAT THEY DO

I want to give you four situations which will demonstrate why this book needed to be written, and should be read by all in order for life to make sense. Let us begin.

Story number 1:

There was a young lady, age 16, named April. One night, when put into a situation of temptation, she failed the test. She allowed things to happen that she knew were not right in an effort to be accepted by her friends, her peers, and in many cases people who wouldn't even come to her funeral if she died. In another location on the same night, there was a young lady of 16 named Julie. Julie was put into the same situation with the same set of friends and with the same choices, but she had something inside of her that would not allow her to go into the world of the defiled, no matter what her friends thought of her. The question is: what does Julie have that April does not have? Both are in the same church; both came from the same Christian home. Many things could be said to have made the difference. You might guess that one is a Christian and the other is not. You might guess that one has had teaching that the other has not had. Yet they are twin sisters, and both of them claim to know God and be known by God. I believe if you will read what I have discovered, you will understand why the two girls (both from the same family and same church, with the same teachers and even baptized the same day), when put into the same situation, responded so differently. Perhaps one is not truly saved. You might guess that, but we find many illustrations from scripture where believers failed on occasions, but were still true believers. Sometimes a believer will fail in one setting but succeed on another day. What makes the difference? I believe I have discovered the answer to these questions.

Story number 2:

Ben, a husband of 12 years, is being pursued by a young woman at his work. He has really struggled, because he and his wife are going through some tough times in their marriage. They have a sick child, his wife is having some health issues, and their personal and private relationship is not what it once was. Yet Ben has continually ignored the advances made by the young co-worker and will continue to do so. Ben lives in a culture where, statistically, six out of 10 married men would fall into sin when placed in these circumstances. Why will Ben make the decision that he will not go down the road of becoming a cheater? I believe if you continue to read what God has allowed me to discover, you will understand.

Story number 3:

In a world where Christianity is not accepted (especially if you are unapologetic about your faith in Jesus Christ as your Savior), a young woman named Asia Bibi was convicted of blasphemy by the Pakistani court, receiving a sentence of death by hanging in 2010. She spent 8 years in prison. During that time her husband and her four daughters, people she loves very dearly, were in hiding because of death threats. Asia appeared before the Islamic-based court 28 times. All she would have had to do to go home and rescue her family from fear and oppression is to confess that Jesus is only a prophet, and not the Son of God or the Savior of the world. All she had to do is declare that Allah is great, and that Mohammed is his prophet, and she would be freed. Even during times when her health was failing and she was not getting proper medical treatment for her issues, she would not deny Christ Jesus. She would not do what would make it easy for her or her family. We must ask ourselves, "Why?"

After reading these situations, I hope that you will continue reading, and find out why some do well (and others not so well) when faced with trials and temptations. Why do some stand firm in their faith and others fail so miserably?

I have discovered that it is all about our level of love for self, others and especially God Himself.

Story number 4 – a biblical example:

King David was deeply in love with God as a young boy and, even after being anointed king and killing the giant Goliath, he patiently waited for God to set the timetable for when he would start to rule as king. He would not harm the present king, Saul, even though King Saul was pursuing him and trying to kill him. Why? Why was David so patient? Because his love for God was bigger than his love for himself. David was placed on the throne at age 40, many years after he was anointed, displaying the fact that love for God gives even a coming king patience. David became a successful warrior and a great king, and even God said that David was a man after the heart of God. However, even David became involved in a forbidden relationship and brought the judgment of God on himself, his family and his nation. The big mystery is how this man who had so much knowledge and so much love for God could find himself in such a place of failure. I submit to you that David fell prey to the struggle we all have: level one love. When you finish reading this observation of the five levels of love, you will understand how this great king could find himself in such misery.

This example declares how one who loves God in an extreme way one day can fall to a low level of love another day, and make terrible mistakes in life that bring grave consequences.

CHAPTER TWO

UNDERSTANDING HOW I CAME TO THIS TRUTH

When God gave Moses the Ten Commandments in Exodus 20, they were a foundation for life. God gave **four commands dealing with our devotion to God, and six dealing with our devotion to others**. There were no declarations for love of self. It seems we already have enough desire to love self. Although love of self is important to be a healthy person, it must come in limited doses. God told us in the Ten Commandments to put God first. In turn, other things would fall into place, especially our ability to deal with other humans. If we settle the issue of who God is, all other issues take care of themselves.

When Jesus was asked by a lawyer in Matthew 22:36-40, *"Master, which is the great commandment in the law?"* Jesus said, *"Thou shalt love* (agape) *the Lord thy God with all thy heart, and with all thy soul, and with all thy mind. This is the first and great commandment. And the second is like unto it, Thou shalt love* (agape) *thy neighbour as thyself. On these two commandments hang all the law and the prophets."*

Everything in life hinges on whether or not we want to fulfill God's will for our lives: love God first, and love others, at the highest level of love -- agape love. As you read on, you will understand Jesus' answer to this lawyer sets the stage for this love-level principle.

When Jesus confronted Simon Peter in John 21, the great question that was asked was about love. "Do you love me more than these?"

Notice the words, "more than these." This shows that there are love levels or love portions. For the sake of understanding, I am calling them love levels or love zones.

As we study this material together, you and I will discover that God told us the key to life on every page of His word, and we have overlooked it for years. **The key to life is love, and the key to understanding love is to understand that love comes in levels!**

CHAPTER THREE

UNDERSTANDING THE WORD "LOVE"

We must first understand the word love. If we believe that all of our relationships hinge on love, we must understand what God taught us about love.

There are many forces in the world, power sources and energy sources, but nothing is more powerful or dictates the acts of an individual like the force called love.

In John 3:16 we have Jesus teaching in a prominently Greek culture. Here He introduced the word "agape" to us as He said, *"For God so loved* (agape) *the world that He gave His only begotten Son, that whosoever believeth in Him should not perish but have everlasting life."* Jesus introduces this element of love here, but God introduced it on the pages of the Old Testament in the life of Abraham (He just did not name it). Here in John's gospel Jesus named it. He called it "agape."

Let us look at Abraham. God asked Abraham to give his son to God and prove his love for Him over all other loves. Here in Genesis chapter 22 God gave us our first look at agape love. God asked Abraham to prove that he loved his Creator more than the gift of his creation (Isaac). Though the word "love" is not mentioned, God was asking Abraham to demonstrate that he loved Him more than his most prized possession on earth. This is clear!

The word love has been so overused that it has almost lost its true meaning. One might say, "I love apple pie," or "I love vanilla ice cream," and really just be making conversation. Love has been the subject of thousands of songs, and the movie industry has certainly mired the truth about love in many ways. It is misused and overused to the point that it is hard to distinguish one's thoughts when using the word.

However, in order to understand what we do and why we do it, we must understand how love dictates to us.

The question in Abraham's life was: how much did he love God, at what was his level of love?

When God called Abraham in Genesis 12, He asked him to love God more than his family. He called Abraham to leave his family and follow God. This was not easy, but as he did it, God knew that Abraham loved Him more.

When the New Testament was penned, the world was under great influence by the Greeks. Alexander the Great and the Greeks had left their mark on the world, spreading the Greek language (this was no accident, as you will see). The Greeks spoke with pointed precision, as you will see declared true in a very special way.

The Greeks have six different words for love, because they wanted you to know exactly what kind of love they were talking about when they spoke or wrote.

- Eros—romantic love or sexual passion-filled love
- Phileo—brotherly or friendship love
- Ludus—playful love
- Pragma—longstanding love
- Philautia—love of self
- Agape—sacrificial love

Each of these words describes a different way of approaching this issue of love. Some have said that God gave the Greeks the influence they had in order to establish the Greek language. Thus, the New Testament would be written in Greek so that God could communicate in a very specific way. Whether this is true or false, the fact remains: God used the Greek language to write His New Testament message. God used the Greek language to describe a few of these love categories. In this study we will try to examine what God intended to do with the issue of love, and gain a better understanding of His intention. Comprehension of the five levels of love will give us a better insight into what drives our own behavior, and the behavior of others.

The two words used most in the New Testament to distinguish between the levels of love are "phileo" (brotherly love) and "agape" (sacrificial love), but there are at least three other levels of love. I personally believe that there are five levels, and we will discuss them.

CHAPTER FOUR
PICTURES OF LOVE LEVELS IN THE BIBLE

We will not discuss every time these levels appear in the Bible, because they are on every page, but we will mention a few.

We have already mentioned Abraham and the clear call for agape-level love in his life, as God asked Abraham for a declaration of love in Genesis 22, the offering of Isaac. Yet when God called him in Chapter 12, He had already asked Abraham to love him more than level two love (which we will define later), because He asked him to leave his family.

We have already mentioned that Jesus declared agape in John 3:16, and continued to declare our need for this level. We will discuss this at length later in this study.

Paul also spoke about certain levels of love!

The Apostle Paul, when writing a letter to the church at Corinth, made some statements about love that are almost unbelievable, except for the fact that he did so by God's order. These words have been read at weddings, been the subject of countless sermons, and used to point to the power of love.

1 Corinthians 13:1-11 *"Though I speak with the tongues of men and of angels and have not charity (agape love), I am become as sounding brass, or a tinkling cymbal. And though I have the gift of prophecy, and understand all mysteries, and all knowledge; and though I have all faith, so that I could remove mountains, and have not charity, I am nothing. And though I bestow all my goods to feed the poor, and though I give my body to be burned, and have not charity, it profiteth me nothing. Charity suffereth long, and is kind; charity envieth not; charity vaunteth not itself, is not puffed up, Doth not behave itself unseemly, seeketh not her own, is not easily provoked, thinketh no evil; Rejoiceth not in iniquity, but rejoiceth in the truth; Beareth all things, hopeth all things, endureth all things. Charity never faileth: but whether there be prophecies, they shall fail; whether there be tongues, they shall cease; whether there be knowledge, it shall vanish away. For we know in part and we prophecy in part. But when that which is perfect is come, then that which is in part shall be done away. When I was a child I spake as a child, I understood as a child, I thought as a child: but when I became a man, I put away childish things."*

When we read this, we read love (charity) never fails; but **Paul was declaring the power of mature love.**

Agape (mature love) is enduring, patient, kind, unselfish, not pride-filled, not easily made angry, does not easily think evil of others, bears all things, hopes for the best, is very enduring. The bottom line is that mature love is a wonderful thing!

Paul is saying that we need love more than we need anything, but not just *any* kind of love. We need <u>mature love</u> because the power of love is in maturity. *"When I was a child, I spoke as child, but when I became mature I put away childish things."* What does this say about the power of love? Paul tells us that there are at least two levels of love, childhood love and mature love. It is important to notice, he is saying that we will not see this wonderful love unless growth takes place and it becomes mature.

Mature love never fails!

When mature love is present, the power is amazing. "Love never fails!" It is not enough to say that love never fails. That is misleading without the rest of the story. Paul did not just say that love never fails. He said that *mature* love (agape love) never fails. What is the difference between agape love and other love? Paul declares here to the Corinthians that agape love is grown, mature love. It was translated "charity" by the King James translators to distinguish the different word here, it seems, but in the Greek it is agape love.

Jesus introduced this love in John 3:16, the most quoted verse in the Bible. Jesus said that this type of love was God's love. When the apostle John wrote the Gospel of John chapter 1:14, he said some challenging words. *"And the Word was made flesh, and dwelt among us, (and we beheld his glory, the glory as of the only begotten of the Father,) full of grace and truth."* The word here for glory is a Greek word that means "to show us who he really is." Therefore, Jesus came down to show us who God really is. He came to show us agape love, God's love. Obviously, God's love is mature love, and never fails.

The level of one's love dictates their every thought, action, success and failure. Our decisions and responses to disappointments all hinge on love, but not *just* love; they hinge on our *level* of love at the time. That is an important distinction: **at the time**.

What did Jesus tell us about love?

In the conversation that took place in John 3 with Nicodemus, Jesus challenged his educated understanding of love. He declared a few things to this religious leader. The love that God has is agape love. Agape gives, agape rescues, agape gives life, and agape pays whatever price is necessary to redeem the souls of men. When one looks at the cross and Christ on it, God is declaring that His love is this big. Jesus told Nicodemus about the level of love that God has for mankind, but Nicodemus had no way of processing such love. Jesus introduced agape love to the world and put it on display. Here in the Gospel of John Chapter 3, Jesus not only introduced this agape love, but He declared what this love looked like. God models this love, as He was willing to send His only begotten Son to die for the rebellious creation of God. This is the greatest picture of agape. When one looks at the cross and the Son of God hanging on it, we have agape on display for the entire world to see.

The most famous verse in the Bible declares this truth in bold letters and in people's hearts. *"For God so loved* (agape) *the world, that He gave His only begotten Son, that whosoever believeth in Him should not perish, but have everlasting life."*

I must point out that the book of Revelation also gives us a picture of this love level on many occasions. The most apparent is the declaration that the church of Ephesus had left its first love. What does that mean? It is a declaration that there are levels of love! Revelation 2:4 *"Nevertheless I have somewhat against thee, because thou hast left thy first love."*

I think you can see God has clearly demonstrated that there are levels of love. I may be taking some liberties here with these levels, but if you will accept the foundation of what I am saying (like Gary Chapman with the love languages), I believe you will see these levels clearly.

Let us discuss the five levels of love that I have discovered in the word of God, and why I believe there are levels. Let us start at level one.

CHAPTER FIVE

EXPLAINING THE FIVE LEVELS OF LOVE

In studying this subject, I see five levels of love that dominate our every move.

We all find ourselves in one level or another all the time, and no one is exempt from the power of love and the zone or level of love we are in at every moment. These love levels dictate our lives! As I study the Bible and study life, I see that there are levels from one to five, one being self-love and five being a love for God. Once I discovered these levels of love in the scriptures, I began to see them in life as well. I began to see how levels of love dictate our every choice.

Level one – what is it?

As we examine level one, we will see that this level can be healthy, but if we *stay* in level one, we will not be healthy for long.

Level one love is the power that moves us to God. Without level one love, we would have no reason to turn to God. We come to God because our sin has put us in a dying position. We are dying by the minute, and we have learned that if we do not come to God in confession and repentance, we will be separated from

God throughout our lives. Even worse, we will spend eternity in a separated state from God in a place where the fallen angels will be for eternity. God has communicated this to us and, in turn, we are driven to God because we love ourselves: level one.

Level one is focused on loving one's self, which is healthy, because it moves us toward God. When one loves self in a healthy way, he or she will be drawn to God, because we will want to live forever instead of die forever. Level one love is self-sustaining love. I contend that we are given level one love by God, in order to give us proper self-worth. It is important for a human to have a healthy self-worth, or he or she suffers in despair and will not even seek to come to God to save themselves. Level one also motivates us to prosper. With a healthy self-worth, one is motivated to set personal goals for life. When one does not possess healthy self-worth (level one love), the motivation to live life is simply not there. However, when it is there, one is motivated to set goals, get an education, become productive and seek to pursue success.

Level one compels us to look for God. As we have mentioned, level one love will motivate one us to make some very important decisions in order to keep from suffering in an afterlife separated from God. God gave us self-love to come to Him for salvation. However, I contend that no human is happy who is not happy with one's self. If we have poor self-esteem, we are not happy people. Tell me, have you ever seen a person that has a poor view of himself happy with anyone or anything? This is why we need parents who believe in us and encourage us to do our best. We need people in our lives who will encourage us to succeed, because we know that they believe in us. A healthy self-worth is needed to be a productive individual. But self-*worship* is not healthy. Level one is good to set a person on the right path, but growing into a person that loves others more than oneself is also a part of producing happiness. If a person stays in level one (self-love) too long, or puts too much emphasis there, it becomes very unhealthy. The relationships of life suffer greatly because life becomes "all about you." Although we must *start* in level one, we must not *stay* in level one. Level one is supposed to bring us to God. Level one is supposed to give us self-worth and self-esteem. Level one is supposed to get our lives going in the right direction. However, level one can become a prison that cages oneself, and punishes anyone who will enters that cage. Level one is designed to push us to God and push us to seek friendships and proper relationships. Yet when level one begins to push others down, and destroy our relationships and our future, we must move up. It is amazing just how bad life becomes when we do not move into level two.

In summary, level one love moves us to happiness. When we possess a healthy self-worth, we just see so much to live for! In that frame of mind, we chose to live a fulfilling life. Healthy love of self gives us confidence to love others; it is difficult to have this type of life without a healthy self-worth (level one).

Level one love motivates us to run from eternal judgment and plead for mercy from God. Level one love is healthy, because it brings us to God. Level one love gives us a healthy look at ourselves. Without level one love (a healthy love for self), we would not be able to love others. We are born with a healthy love of self, and that is God's design, but level one love is not to be as far as we go. If we stop at level one, we become self-centered and selfish to the point of misery, both four ourselves and everyone around us. Please understand, level one love is needed at the beginning, and is healthy in life, but if that is as far as we go in love, we become most miserable.

We see level one love dominating the baby Christian who is simply asking God to do something for them (not wanting to do anything for others or even for God). This is the danger of staying in the zone of level one, even after we become believers in Christ. Simply put, our churches are filled with level one Christians, only after the milk of the word, only wanting God to serve them and never moving to serve Him nor anyone else. This produces a group of believers who are going to heaven when they die, but will have very little to show for their life here on earth.

We are to start life with level one, but as we grow, we must progress to level two.

Level two – what is it?

Both levels one and two were declared boldly by Jesus in Luke 15:11-32, the parable of the lost son. This parable is all about the love that the Father had for his son, which is level two love. Level two is when you move from love of self to loving your family or someone close to you more than you love yourself. We recognize this move by the way we are willing to sacrifice self for that person. When we move to level two, we will put them above ourselves. In Luke 15, the prodigal son was stuck in level one (self-love), but the Father displayed level two love by his willingness to give the inheritance to his son, even though it was not time. One doesn't get the inheritance from the parent until the parent dies, but here the father loved the son enough to put himself out of the way and give to the son. The youngest son finally came to his senses and realized just how valuable his father was to him. He returned to the father and declared that he was not worthy to be called his son. He put himself aside to honor the father. The oldest brother then came into the picture. He, too, was in level one, as he was not happy that the brother had returned. As we read the story of the prodigal, we see level one and level two in a clear picture.

We hope that we see level two come to a relationship when we marry our sweetheart. In counseling sessions as a Pastor, I have asked many young men why they wanted to marry the sweet girl who sat with them. Many times I have gotten statements like, "She makes me feel good," or, "She is a great cook," etc., which is actually love of self, level one love. They simply are marrying their bride because of what she can do for them. This is not level two love. Level two love is seen in a marriage when we want to serve the spouse, not be served by the spouse.

This is also clearly seen in becoming a parent. When we become parents, we become servants to our children. We become parents because we want someone to love more than we love ourselves, typically. We know we have moved to level two when we are willing to sacrifice for someone other than ourselves. We know that we have moved to level two when we are willing to put ourselves aside for those in our level two love zone. We then *know* we are at level two. We might *think* we are at level two when we fall in love with someone and even marry them, but unless we are willing to put their needs above our own, we are marrying to serve ourselves or to be served -- level one.

Understanding how level two motivates us and declares us

This love is modeled as a father or mother gets up before sunrise and goes to work in cold weather, even though he or she would love to stay in bed. Why? Because we have a family that we must care for. This is modeled as parents get up in the middle of the night to feed and change a child, even though the parent can hardly sit up for lack of sleep. This is also modeled as a teenager comes home from a party early because he or she did not want to disappoint their parents, even though selfish level one wanted to stay at the party. Their level two love compels them on that day or night to come home on time, to honor his or her parents.

Understanding what happens if we never reach level two

When people do not reach level two, and they are consumed with their own needs, their own will, their own satisfaction, they hurt the people in their world. Consequently, in the end, they destroy their own happiness. They lose the very thing they sacrificed everyone else to gain. I once knew of a mother who ran away with a man and left her husband, her children and her parents. She left all the people she said she loved for a man she thought she loved more than anyone. She would tell her children she loved them, but her actions showed that she thought she loved another man more than them. Some would say she loved the new man more than her family, but I contend that she loved herself and the life she had with this new man. Her happiness was more important to her than her family's happiness, and her actions clearly displayed that. But the things she thought she had to have would come back to hurt her, as they always do when you act out in level one, and hurt those you have promised to love at level two.

I hope you can think about your own illustrations of levels one and two, and how to spot each level. It will make life much easier when you can understand this principle. If nothing else, it will keep us from moving back to level one and destroying our families and our own future happiness.

I am sure that just understanding levels one and two answers many questions. I heard just today, as I was writing this, of a young wife and mother who just told her husband that she had met someone else, and that she would be moving out. She said the children would understand in time. I wonder: did this bride ever get to level two, or was she always on level one? That is a good question, but I contend that she could have very well been at level two when she got married and when she had children. What is clear today is that, if she *was* at level two, she is truly not *today*; she is clearly stuck in level one, an unhealthy level one.

Level three – what is it?

Level three love is all about loving people we do not even know. This is mission love. God has commissioned His followers to go to all the world and tell the story of the death, burial and resurrection of Christ Jesus. There is no other way for the world to trust the work of God in their lives so He can forgive their sins and save them from certain separation from Himself. However, for us to be willing to obey this commission there must be something bigger than level two love. This is clearly another level of love. This level is shown when we love people we do not know more than we love our own families. My own personal story is one of leaving behind my beloved family and living somewhere that was not my home. I had to get to know strangers, simply because I felt that God told me to go and live there as a Pastor. However, I have heard stories of missionaries who left the states, went to some foreign land, and had to leave their children in a mission school hours and even sometimes days away from them in order to minister to strangers, simply because God said to do so. This is a step up from level two, because we are clearly demonstrating a level of love that is greater than our love for our families. **This is level three!**

The Apostle Paul best illustrated level three love when he said he would be willing to be accursed to see his people saved. I am sure Paul was talking about the Jewish nation, but we all know that Paul did not know every one of the Jewish people of the nation. He called them his people. This demonstrates what I believe is level three. Paul declared that he would be willing to be cursed for the people he loved, though he did not personally know "his people." He demonstrated that he loved his mission calling more than himself, and more than his previous life. This is what I call level three.

Romans 9: 1-3 *"I say the truth in Christ, I lie not, my conscience also bearing me witness in the Holy Ghost, That I have great heaviness and continual sorrow in my heart. For I could wish that myself were accursed from Christ for my brethren, my kinsmen according to the flesh."*

Level three love is what empowers missions. The mission of the New Testament church cannot be something we just do because Jesus tells us to. We are moved by God, called by God, to go and do missions because love level three moves into our hearts and moves us to do so. Level three love is a God-granted gift and calling for sure. It simply makes no earthly sense otherwise. Are you getting an understanding of mission-motivated level three?

A Christian approach to level three

Level three for the Christian is being willing to leave everything and go to a place where you may need to be uncomfortable because of a calling that is in your heart. It is a calling to love a people you do not know more than you love yourself and more that you love your level two parents, friends and even wife and/or children. As you can tell, I believe level three love does not occur naturally -- it takes God to make it happen. Level three love is a product of God's heart becoming part of who we are, because God truly had level three love. When He came here to die for the sins of the world, we were a people who did not know Him at the time, but He came to die anyway.

When we give money to a missionary cause to purchase shoes or clothing, food or medicine for people we do not know (nor will we ever meet on this side of heaven), something has happened in our hearts when we see or hear about a need. We are moved to take away from our family and ourselves and give for a stranger. This is a step above level two; this is level three and it is very real. There would be very little mission work done, very few hospitals built, very few missionaries sent, without level three love.

A Secular look at level three

It is hard for someone who is stuck in level one or level two to understand level three. When a level one and level two person hears that someone has left a thriving medical practice to go to the jungle where there is little to no money, and they even have to raise their own support, the level one and level two person cannot do this at all. Level one cannot identify with this because of the discomfort and uncertainty that comes with level three love. The level two people are thinking about leaving family to go and do this work, and they cannot imagine it. Many will not even allow themselves to consider level three because they are so set in level one or two. I am not saying that everyone should leave the states and go to the jungles; I am just trying to get our readers to understand how and why level three happens, and why levels one and two will not even think about such a thing. However, many of us cannot go (nor are we called to go), but we *are* all called to be involved in level three missions, because our Lord told us that if we are to be obedient servants we would, in some way, be moved to get involved in level three missions. We may not be the ones to go, but we will be the one to send them. Not everyone can go. Some people need to stay home and build a strong body of believers to support those who are called to go, but we are all called to be involved in level three in some way. This is simply the process of growing as a believer: growing from level one to level two, and then being involved in level three, missions.

Could level three just be level one in costume?

Level three can be level one dressed up to look good. If someone chose to participate in a mission project but had a selfish motive, they may look like level three, but their motive actually says level one. Therefore, motive determines when one is experiencing level one, two or three. It is all about motive and, many times, God is the only one who really knows.

The importance of level three

Level three is important for the proclaiming of the gospel of Christ. Jesus was counting on many people being willing to move to level three as He gave the Great Commission. If no one ever reached level three, missions would never have happened, but God calls us to level three. In level three, one is willing to give to someone he or she may never see this side of heaven, but sacrifices are made anyway. This is level three, loving people we do not even know, sacrificing for people that we do not know, and doing so in a way that no one knows but God. It's something that, sometimes, we do not even understand ourselves

Level three is declared clearly in Luke 10:25-37, the story of the Good Samaritan. This is a story of a man who found a stranger beaten on the side of the road.

Even though he did not know him, he carried him to an inn, paid for his medicine, and arranged to have him cared for while he was gone. Remember, he did not know the hurt man, but he loved a perfect stranger enough to sacrifice for him. However, neither the Priest nor the Levite loved this stranger enough to sacrifice for him. You might ask why these two men would walk right by this man and do nothing, knowing he was in need of help. While we could speculate about their going to the temple and not wanting to become defiled, I contend that the bottom line is that these two had level one love all the way. At this point in our study, we should be able to see that. This story gives us a clear picture of what level three love looks like. A stranger lay beaten on the side of the road and this Samaritan showed him love and kindness -- all for no reason but something in his heart. **The only explanation is that he was compelled by level three love! This was a love above self and above family and friends. The next level!**

Level four – what is it?

Level four is Samaritan love. Not the *Good Samaritan* love, but the "go" command. We are to go to the Samaritans, a step up from levels one, two and three. This takes more love than level three. It is a step up -- a more mature love. When in level three, we are ministering to strangers, but in level four we will be ministering to our enemies.

We must be willing to love our enemies in order to go to them and proclaim the gospel. Is that not what Jesus told His people to do, to love their enemy? He told them to feed their enemy, pray for them, do good to them. In Matthew 5:43-48 Jesus told His followers, *"Ye have heard that it hath been said, Thou shalt love thy neighbour, and hate thine enemy. But I say unto you, Love your enemies, bless them that curse you, do good to them that hate you, and pray for them which despitefully use you, and persecute you; That ye may be the children of your Father which is in heaven: for he maketh his sun to rise on the evil and on the good, and sendeth rain on the just and on the unjust. For if you love them which love you, what reward have ye? do not even the publicans the same? And if ye salute your brethren only, what do ye more than others? do not even the publicans so? Be ye therefore perfect, even as your Father which is in heaven is perfect."*

Jesus is calling on His followers to step up and not to just *minister,* to them but minister to them because you *love* them.

Just before He went to heaven, Jesus said in Acts 1:8 *"But ye shall receive power, after that the Holy Ghost is come upon you: and ye shall be witnesses unto me* *both in Jerusalem, and in all Judaea, **and in Samaria,** and unto the uttermost part of the earth."*

We are talking about the Samaritans. Most of the time we read the Great Commission and we just read right over this word, Samaria, but Samaritans were people that these disciples hated. They thought the Samaritans were animals, unclean half-breeds. They wanted nothing to do with them. They would walk miles out of the way just to keep from walking through Samaria. I am sure these words came as a shock to the disciples. They had gone through Samaria a few times, but now Jesus was actually telling them that they needed to take the gospel story to the land of the Samaritans. Remember that these disciples were all Jewish men who had nothing to do with the Samaritans.

Level four love has matured to be able to overcome racism. The whole world has suffered with some form of racism. I have been in many countries, and I have been hard-pressed to find a people group that doesn't have some form of racism. However, racism can be overcome if we move to level four, and Jesus is saying that His followers should be able to get to this level. We know we are at level four when we come to love those we do not even like. Jesus told us to love our enemies, pray for them and do good to those who despitefully use us. In order to be able to carry out this command of Christ we must grow to level four, loving your enemies. He said anyone could love those who are good to him or her, but His followers would be able to love their enemies. After the Tower of Babel, God divided and dispersed the nations giving them different languages; miles and years separated them. They became influenced by hurts and grave disagreements. When they got back together, it was hard not to be influenced by past hurts, past wars and past issues, to the point that some began to consider those of another race their enemy. Yet God is saying that His people can overcome all of these issues and go to them in love. This has to be a new level, level four. Notice, He said that after the Holy Ghost came upon us, we would be witnesses to the Samaritans. It is clear Jesus knew that if we were to love our enemies, it would take the presence of God to help us move to level four.

In the gospel commission, we have the command to go and share out of concern for our enemies and those we do not like, but I contend that this was not new. God called Jonah to go to his enemies and give them a message that would cause them to repent and save them from judgment. In his heart, however, Jonah wanted them under the judgment of God, so he would not go to them in level four love. God made Jonah go, but he went because of level one love only. When Jonah was in the belly of the whale, he was crying out for deliverance, saying that if God would deliver him, he would deliver the message; that is exactly what happened. However, after Jonah delivered the message, he sat down to watch the people he did not like be placed under the mighty judging hand of God. Instead, they repented and God gave them mercy, and you may remember that Jonah got upset at God for their repentance and the mercy extended to them. Jonah was at level one all the way!

Level five – what is it?

Level five is a big step up from level four, and an enormous step up from level one.

In John 21:15, while sitting by the fire, Jesus asked Peter, *"Simon, son of Jonas, lovest thou me more than these?"*

Jesus said in Luke 14:26-35, *"If any man come to me, and hate not his father, and mother, and wife, and children, and brethren, and sisters, yea, and his own life also, he cannot be my disciple. And whosoever doth not bear his cross, and come after me, cannot be my disciple. For which of you intending to build a tower, sitteth not down first and counteth the cost, whether he have sufficient to finish it? Lest haply, after he hath laid the foundation, and is not able to finish it, all that behold it begin to mock him, Saying, This man began to build and was not able to finish. Or what king, going to make war against another king, sitteth not down first, and consulteth whether he be able with ten thousand to meet him that cometh against him with twenty thousand? Or else, while the other is yet a great way off, he sendeth an ambassage, and desireth conditions of peace. So likewise, whosoever he be of you that forsaketh not all that he hath, he cannot be my disciple."*

When we read this, unless we understand what level five love is all about, it is hard to understand how anyone, including Jesus, could say that a person should love Him more than our own mother, our children, even our own life. However, we now understand that love has levels. Mature love is agape love, and agape love is not about you. Level five love is a love reserved for God alone. **That is the kind of love that never fails -- level five -- modeled by Jesus and expected of His servants. Level five love is what He is asking for from His followers.** This is why He said what He did in Luke 14:26-35, and ended by saying that if we could not rise to this level of love and the commitments this kind of love produces, we could not be His disciple. A disciple is a follower; if we do not love at this level, we cannot follow Him to some of the places He is going to take us.

Jesus knew that He was going to send his disciples into places they would not be willing to go without level five love. Jesus knew that many of His followers would be persecuted, even killed, for simply being a part of His world.

John 15:18-19 *"If the world hate you, ye know that it hated me before it hated you. If ye were of the world, the world would love his own: but because ye are not of the world, but I have chosen you out of the world, therefore the world hateth you."*

This is the love level that Jesus modeled as He went to the Garden of Gethsemane and cried out to the Father, *"Not my will but thine be done."* Jesus did not want to go to the cross, but He loved His Father too much not to be willing to go. He did it, not so much for mankind, but for God the Father. You might say that Jesus was battling level one love and level five love in the Garden of Gethsemane, as He did not want to have to go to the cross. He cried out to the father for another way (if another way existed), but as you know, He came to level five and said, "Not my will but thine." Level five won the day. This scene has played out in the heart of the disciple for the last 2,000 years as many martyrs have shown willingness to die rather than save their own lives. **This is Level five!**

You will remember that, in our introduction, we discussed two girls: Julie and April. One fell to peer pressure, but one stood firm.

When understanding these principles, we can see how Julie could respond in a completely different way than her sister, April, when confronted with the same circumstances. Julie was at least in level two love. Julie did not want to disappoint her mom and dad. Maybe she was even at level five and did not want to disappoint God, her Heavenly Father, by failing to resist temptation. Either way, she would not allow herself to do like her sister. WHAT WAS THE DIFFERENCE? One sister was at level one only and the other was at least at level two or maybe even level five. Either way, she was not at level one like her sister.

We also can understand why Ben will not fall into the arms of the young woman at the office, even though he is tempted to do so. He is at least at level two, but perhaps at level five. Remember the story of Joseph in Genesis 39 as he said to Potiphar's wife as she seduced him, "How then can I do this great wickedness, and sin against God?" Joseph displayed level five love in Genesis 39 and went to prison for it.

Now we can understand why Asia Bibi will not deny Jesus and go home to her family. She is at level five for sure, and chooses not go down the road of disappointing her Heavenly Father.

We now can understand what happened to King David. David was writing love letters to God for most of his life, but one afternoon, he brought nothing but embarrassment to himself, his family and the kingdom of Israel.

And now we can understand why God gave two sets of commandments, the first four pointing to our relationship with God, and the other six addressing our relationship to humans. Remember, Jesus told his followers that if they could get their relationships with God and man right, they would be in good shape.

These are some of the most challenging words in the Bible, but if we understand these five love levels, we can understand these words. Jesus wanted us to grow to level five so we would be able to go places where He would send us. He wants us to grow to level five so we can trusted to do what He wants us to do. He can trust those who love God more than self, family, money, fame, even life.

We are told to grow in grace and in the knowledge of the Lord Jesus Christ, and in turn, we grow in our love to level five.

No matter the time or the place, when one of Jesus' disciples is put into a place of sacrifice, it takes level five to be willing to pay the price.

This was why John 21 was Simon Peter's "come to Jesus" meeting. Simon was tested in Gethsemane. He failed the test, it seems, because he got his feelings hurt over the scolding he took for taking up the sword.

He seemed to just back up in confusion. It looked like Simon was willing to die for Jesus, just as he had said in the upper room; but when scolded, he went back to level one and then denied that he even knew Jesus. Many times, when we disappoint others, God, and ourselves we cannot imagine why we made such a mistake. Yet if the truth is known, we left our first love! As Jesus told the church at Ephesus in Revelation 2, the first love here was agape love, level five love.

Revelations 2:1-5 *"Unto the angel of the church Ephesus write; These things saith he that holdeth the seven stars in his right hand, who walketh in the midst of the seven golden candlesticks. I know thy works, and thy labour, and thy patience, and how thou canst not bear them which are evil: and thou hast tried them which say they are apostles, and are not, and hast found them liars: And hast borne, and hast patience, and from my name's sake hast laboured, and hast not fainted. Nevertheless I have somewhat against thee, because thou hast left thy first love. Remember therefore from whence thou art fallen, and repent, and do the first works; or else I will come unto thee quickly, and will remove thy candlestick out of his place, except thou repent."*

When we grasp this level five love, we understand the seriousness of this. God wants His people and His churches to love God at level five, or we fail and lose our blessings before the Lord Jesus.

After He rose from the dead, Jesus appeared to the disciples during the course of forty days. During one of these occurrences, the disciples asked, *"...wilt thou at this time restore again the kingdom to Israel?"* (Acts 1:6). They were displaying level one love. Jesus answered them, *"It is not for you to know the times or the seasons, which the Father hath put in his own power."* He steered their focus from themselves (level one), back to the Father (level five).

John 21 stands as the declaration of what Jesus wanted from Simon Peter. Jesus knew that Simon Peter was not going to be able to fulfill his destiny without level five love. Therefore, Jesus was compelling him to rise up to that level. As He compelled him, it is interesting to note that Jesus continually told him to feed His sheep. Jesus was calling Simon to love, and this love would bring him to be willing to push beyond himself, serve Jesus with his life, and serve others, no matter the cost to himself.

John 21:18 *"Verily, verily, I say unto thee, When thou wast young thou, girdest thyself, and walkest whither thou wouldest: but when thou shalt be old, thou shalt stretch forth thy hands, and another shall gird thee, and carry thee whither thou wouldest not."* He spoke of the manner in which Peter would be put to death.

Then Jesus said to him *"Follow Me,"* (v 19). In light of this daunting future, Peter faltered back to level one love, asking in verse 21 what would happen to John. Jesus redirected him to a higher level once again in verse 22, *"If I will that he tarry till I come, what is that to thee? Follow thou me."*

This is all about taking Peter to where he will be the servant that he can be, but only if he can go to agape (level five) and stay there.

CHAPTER SIX

WHY "APPLE EATING" IN GENESIS CHAPTER THREE IS CALLED "THE FALL"

As you and I discover the different levels of love, we can understand how the level of love we are in each day dictates our decisions. The level at that moment will determine what we do. When I discovered these levels in the scriptures, I could finally understand how and why people do what they do. Every decision is made in light of what level we happen to be in that day and in particular, at that moment. This is simply an amazing discovery! Adam and Eve's decision to eat the "apple" was not just something that happened. In order for Eve to eat that fruit, she had to leave level five and drop into level one. It seems the serpent worked on her for a long period of time. He convinced her that God did not want her to eat this fruit because it would give her the ability to be like Him. He claimed God was simply keeping her down by withholding the fruit from her. As long as she loved the creator at a level five, she would not eat the fruit; but when she was convinced that God was holding out on her, she left level five and went to level one. In turn, she ate the fruit in disobedience. I believe, after discovering this principle, that her love for self was the reason she failed; and in order for her to fall to love self over God, she had to demonize God in her mind. This is a very valuable lesson for us all. We must be very careful not to demonize others, especially those we are supposed to love above ourselves. **Eve fell from level five to level one,** and that is the reason it is called "the fall." She fell in her heart from her worship of God and turned her worship toward self, level one.

Even the devil himself fell from five to one. From what we know about the angel Lucifer, he decided that he wanted to be like the Most High, and declared himself to be in level one. When this took place, he was able to convince a third of the created angels in heaven to move to level one as well. Consequently, God had to put Lucifer and all those who followed him out of heaven. Therefore, even heaven is affected by these levels.

CHAPTER SEVEN

DISCUSSING WHY PEOPLE DO WHAT THEY DO IN LIGHT OF THE FIVE LEVELS

This question is easily answered when we understand these levels and how they affect our lives.

We understand **Eve went from level five to level one** and fell from favor. I believe that **Adam ate the fruit out of level two love**. You might ask why I would think such a thing, but in the big picture of chapters 2 and 3 of Genesis we must understand what would have happened if Eve was defiled by disobedience and Adam was still pure. God would have had to remove Eve from Adam. It is hard to think about it, but God could not leave them together if Adam did not eat the fruit. Adam ate the fruit out of level two love. Adam loved Eve more that he loved himself and, in turn, became defiled along with her so he could stay with her -- level two love! Each one of us walks the road of love levels each minute of each hour of each day. How we respond when something comes into our world of temptation depends on where our level is at that moment.

Think of Simon Peter on the day Jesus asked, *"Whom do men say that I the Son of man am?"* (Matthew

16:13), and then in verse 15, *"But whom say ye that I am?"* Simon Peter said, *"Thou are the Christ, the Son of the living God."* Jesus commented on how God had to tell him that. As we read further in Matthew 16, we find Simon Peter telling Jesus that he would not stand for Him being arrested and crucified. Jesus had to scold him for his harsh talk. Also, on the night of the last supper, when Jesus said that one of them would betray Him, the disciples were all asking if it was them, but Simon Peter did not ask that. Instead, he declared that he would stick to Jesus, go to prison with Him if necessary, or even die for Jesus. Yet a few hours later he was denying that he even knew Jesus. Why, and how does understanding the five levels of love help us answer the question why?

In the middle of the final Passover meal, Jesus introduced the communion meal. He looked over at Peter, and said (Luke 22:31-34), *"...Simon, Simon, behold, Satan hath desired to have you, that he may sift you as wheat: But I have prayed for thee, that thy faith fail not: and when thou art converted strengthen thy brethren. And he said unto Him, Lord, I am ready to go with the, both into prison, and to death. And he (Jesus) said, I tell thee, Peter, the cock shall not crow this day, before that thou shall thrice deny, that thou knowest me."*

What does all that mean?

Jesus knew that while in His presence at the table, Peter believed that his love was at level five. However, Jesus knew that after a few events, Simon Peter would go right back to level one and he would deny Him. I believe we can see that Simon Peter meant every word that he said when he claimed to be willing to die for Jesus. But I also believe we can see that, after Jesus scolded him for cutting the man's ear off, and telling him that He did not need him to fight for Him, **Simon dropped from level five to level one in a moment.** He ran away, and when he resurfaced, he was in level one and denied Jesus, even three times. Why? Level one! You see, we live in the victory in our walk as long as we are in level five love, but if our enemy (or simply life's challenges) can get our love to turn to self, we are going to make a mess. Level one love is not a place we should stay in long. Level one is the level of devastation. Jesus did not give up on Simon Peter, but helped him grow out of this inconsistency. When Jesus talked to Simon in John 21, after the denial, He pressed Simon to move to level five and stay there. This would solve the problem of inconsistent service. This, in turn, would allow Peter to <u>be converted, enabling him to strengthen his brethren, as instructed in Luke 22</u>.

Think about Judas Iscariot. Judas was a man who was raised in the home of a leper, his father being Simon the Leper. In John 12 Jesus attended a celebration that took place after Lazarus was raised from death in John 11. If you read this, you will notice that this is the place and time that Judas was upset because of the ointment that was poured over Jesus' feet. Judas was complaining about the waste of it. Learning this, I have come to believe that Judas was with Jesus for one reason and for one reason only: Judas wanted power and recognition. Growing up in the house of Simon the Leper, Judas was probably outcast by society. Power and money would give him personal recognition. (moved from p 25)

We have always been pretty hard on Judas Iscariot and Simon Peter, but they were just people who went into level one and made a big mess. We do not know if Judas was ever anywhere *but* level one, but we truly can see that when he betrayed Jesus, he was at level one. Yet after the fact, when he saw Jesus being treated in such a bad way, he wanted level five at that point. Then we see him move away from what he was doing. Some would argue, however, that he went back to level one when he hung himself, not wanting to live with such a devastating decision. Interesting thoughts: and these levels help us evaluate these very devastating decisions.

I have a theory that I would like to share; I believe it will give insight into both of the disciples.

Both Judas and Simon Peter became offended at Jesus, leading them to do what they did. <u>When offense comes, we lose our levels</u>. Offense is a big feeder of level one. It is hard to be offended and stay away from level one. When Judas was offended by Jesus' words in Simon the Leper's house about the ointment and the money, he went out and "sold" Jesus. When Simon was scolded for cutting off the man's ear at Gethsemane, he was offended and did not follow closely when Jesus was arrested. Before morning, he had denied Him three times.

Beware: offense is a level five destroyer. We must refuse to be offended in order to get to *and stay at* level five, or any other level except level one.

CHAPTER EIGHT

HOW TO DISCOVER YOUR LOVE LEVEL

How can I discover my level? Am I willing to admit the truth about where I am? It is important to note that we move from one level to another, sometimes often, but we can evaluate ourselves as to what level we are in most often.

Our love levels can move from level one to level five and level five to level one. This can happen from day to day, minute to minute, and even event to event. We have looked into one of the best examples of this as we examine Simon Peter's great betrayal. With this knowledge, we can understand how Jesus could be betrayed by the man some would call His best friend. Remember, Simon Peter, when in the upper room with Jesus having the Passover/Communion meal, was making great claims about how he was willing to die for Jesus. However, when the time came for him to die for Jesus, he ran away. Simon Peter had declared that he had the kind of love for Jesus that would compel him to suffer anything for Jesus. As he spoke in the upper room, it seems he felt he had level five love. We all want to be at level five! We may be there Sunday morning, in in the middle of worship service; but when we get out in the real world, depending on our circumstances, we may not be at level five for long. Level five is where we want to be and where we want to stay. God wants us at level five because level five love, as we know, never fails. As Paul told the Corinthian Christians, in 1 Corinthians 13:1-13 *"Though I speak with the tongues of men and of angels, and have not charity* (agape love)*, I am become as sounding brass, or a tinkling cymbal. And though I have the gift of prophecy, and understand all mysteries, and all knowledge; and though I have all faith, so that I could remove mountains, and have not charity* (agape)*, I am nothing. And though I bestow all my goods to feed the poor, and though I give my body to be burned, and have not charity* (agape)*, it profiteth me nothing. Charity* (agape) *suffereth long, and is kind; charity* (agape) *envieth not; charity* (agape) *vaunteth not itself, is not puffed up. Doth not behave itself unseemly, seeketh not her own, is not easily provoked, thinketh no evil; Rejoiceth not in iniquity, but rejoiceth in the truth; Beareth all things, believeth all things, hopeth all things, endureth all things. Charity* (agape) *never faileth: but whether there be prophecies, they shall fail; whether there be tongues, they shall cease; whether there be knowledge, it shall vanish away. For we know in part, and we prophecy in part. But when that which is perfect is come, then that which is in part shall be done away. When I was a child, I spake as a child, I understood as a child, I thought as a child: but when I* *became a man, I put away childish things. For now we see through a glass, darkly; but then face to face: now I know in part; but then shall I know even as also I am known. And now abideth faith, hope, charity* (agape)*, these three; but the greatest of these is charity* (agape)*."*

But how do I discover what my love level is? It is really determined by a person's willingness to sacrifice and suffer. If we are willing to suffer for Jesus, we are at level five; if we aren't, we are not there. It is that simple. Level five is where Jesus wants us to be, but being there and *staying there* is the greatest challenge in life.

It is great reading John 14, 15 and 16. As Jesus was on His way to Gethsemane, He said this very clearly many times in these three chapters, "If you love (agape) Me, you will keep My commands; and if you do, My Father will open heaven to you." Read these three chapters with this in mind, and you will see them in a fresh way.

CHAPTER NINE

MOVING FROM LEVEL ONE TO LEVEL FIVE

It is wonderful to say that we want to move from level one to level five, but how do we do that?

The psalmist, David, is a prime example of how to move oneself up the scale to level five. We have already mentioned David, and how he was a great example to us. We must also refer to the great Apostle Paul. After his conversion on the road to Damascus, he displayed level five in a big way, as he told what motivated him to do what he was doing. 2 Corinthians 5:14 *"For the love of Christ constraineth us..."* Notice, he said the love of Christ *constrains*. Paul was moved by the love of Christ. Some would argue that Paul was not talking about his love for Christ but that Christ's love was in him and moved him. Yet, when we examine the life of Paul, we must conclude that Paul loved Jesus Christ more than he love his own life. Paul was in love with Jesus because Jesus loved him enough to forgive his terrible sin debt. That is where level five love must begin -- with the love of Christ for us -- and then our gratitude moves us to love Him more than we love ourselves. In 1 John 4:19 John writes, *"We love him, because he first loved us."* That is where we must start. In the book of Romans, we see the other side of love. In Romans 1:21 he said, *"Because that, when they knew God, they glorified Him not as God, neither were thankful; but became vain in their imaginations, and their foolish heart was darkened."*

All this is interesting and educational, but I must point out that people who live in countries where their lives are threatened when they become believers go from level one to level five at once, because they have no choice. When they come to the knowledge of their need of Christ's payment for their sin, they know that Jesus paid for their sin debt. They also know, however, that they may be called on to make a sacrifice as well when they come to believe. Their sacrifice would not be to pay for their sin, but to prove their level five love. It is interesting to consider the question as to why they come to level five so fast; most of us in comfortable environments come so slowly (and some never come to the five level at all). All I can say is that Jesus was very clear about His expectation of all His followers. He warned His followers as He walked to the Garden of Gethsemane that they would be the enemy of the world, because they were friends with Him. John 15:18-21 *"If the world hate you, ye know that it hated me before it hated you. If ye were of the world, the world would love his own: but because ye are not of the world, but I have chosen you out of the world, therefore the world hateth you. Remember the word that I said unto you, The servant is not greater than his lord. If they have persecuted me, they will also persecute you; if they have kept my saying, they will keep yours also. But all these things will they do unto you for my name's sake, because they know not him that sent me."* John 16: 1 *"These things have I spoken unto you, that ye should not be offended."*

It seems that those who are willing to die for their faith are focusing on the mercy shown to them. They are just grateful to be a part of the kingdom world, and are willing to die to do so. Extreme gratitude is the only explanation for their going from level one to level five immediately. That is the only thing that is different. Therefore, we learn that level five is a product of gratitude.

Jesus expected the world to reject all His friends. He told His friends to expect rejection, and be willing to be persecuted because of Him. However, we in the prosperous nations do not expect to have our relationship challenged. In suppressed countries, their "Bible college education" and respectability many times is determined by how many times they have been to prison for Jesus, or just how much they have had to suffer for Him. This is what I contend is level five, and this is what Jesus wanted for us all.

The Apostle Paul instructed his friend and partner in the ministry, Timothy, as Paul prepared himself to be martyred for the faith 2 Tim. 2:11b-12 *"if we be dead with Him, we shall also live with him. If we suffer, we shall also reign with him: if we deny him, he also will deny us:"* and 3:12 *"Yea, and all that will live godly in Christ Jesus shall suffer persecution."*

CHAPTER TEN

UNDERSTANDING HOW MOVING FROM ONE LEVEL TO ANOTHER AFFECTS OUR LIVES

We have already answered this question, but we need to emphasize this struggle in a big way, because it has such big consequences. We have discovered that we can change levels each day, each hour or even each event. However, this is not a healthy way to walk the road with Christ Jesus, and it is not what He wants for us. In order to be healthy, I must focus on trying to move from level one to level five. It is clear that Jesus wanted Peter on level five as He continued to challenge his love level in John 21. Jesus wants us at a consistent level five. It is like our blood sugar numbers, or our blood pressure or even our heart rate. There are healthy levels for these measurements; if we are at certain numbers, we are considered healthy. If those numbers are off, however, so is our health. Jesus wanted us at level five, and I would say we need to try to get to level five and stay there. As we have mentioned already, David went from level five to level one and committed adultery with Bathsheba, bringing devastation on his family and his kingdom.

David had spent his life loving God through songs and writings to God. When he sinned with Bathsheba, though, he sent his neighbor (a committed soldier) to the front line to be killed, because he had fallen to level one. This is the only explanation for this act of sin. This act was filled with many sins, but these many sins were only possible because of one thing: level one.

Let us discuss the brothers of Jesus. In John 7, we see that Jesus' own half-brothers did not believe in Him; instead, they made very sarcastic comments about Him. After the crucifixion and resurrection, they changed. James, His half-brother, became the pastor of the church in Jerusalem, and Jude, also the half-brother of Jesus, became a believer and wrote the book of Jude. They both completely changed and were willing to die for Jesus if necessary.

There is story after story, but it all comes down to the question of what is your number today? Love level numbers are the things that will dictate what we will and will not do.

CHAPTER ELEVEN

UNDERSTANDING HOW OUR LOVE LEVEL AFFECTS THE DECISIONS WE MAKE FROM ONE DAY TO THE NEXT

It is important to learn to think in terms of these levels. Let us examine together a few biblical stories and see if you can gauge the level of love when decisions were made. I know we have already mentioned a few, and as we go through the Bible stories we may mention them again, but we must examine them in light of this knowledge.

Biblical examples

We have mentioned David, but let us discover the rest of the story:

David, the king of Israel, is well known for writing many of the Psalms of the Bible, became a very beloved king in Israel in the Old Testament books of 1 and 2 Samuel, and is listed in the Kings and Chronicles. He had a wonderful love for God the Father, which is shown in the many Psalms he wrote. God Himself even recorded that David was a man that was after God's own heart, which indicates that David had gotten to the level five state according to God. One day, David was home and not with his men, as he had been many times. He was spending leisure time at home, went up to his house's roof and saw his neighbor's wife taking a bath. At that moment, instead of his love for God (level five), David immediately slipped to level one, and ordered that she be brought to him. After David had committed this level one sin, he continued to live in that level one zone for a long time. When the prophet, Nathan, came to him and challenged him with the truth, David's heart was shaken, and he repented. Most would say that he sought the level five position again, and it took him a long time to get there. Psalms 51 is his plea before God to get back the joy of the level five relationship with God. An issue David had for years with women finally manifested itself into a destructive level-one assault on David and on his level five love for God. It is apparent that we are very powerful in battle when we are at level five, but our enemy is constantly trying to take us back to level one and into the area of self-love and self-worship.

Examining David helps us to understand that it is possible to go back after dropping levels, but we must guard against this, because the devastation caused when going back to level one is enormous. It is good to love your family more than yourself, and it is good to love a specific mission endeavor, but when we go back to level one, it can become very destructive. It is also important to note that it took confession and repentance to get David back to desiring level five again.

Let's discuss the problem caused when a lower level is more important than the highest level.

When we love our spouse, our children, or even our parents more than we love missions or God, we will not be willing to go and serve if we are called to go away from our family.

Think on this: if Abraham would have loved his family more than God, he would never have followed God's call. If Peter and the disciples would not have loved Jesus at a high level, they would not have followed Him to be fishers of men. God calls His followers to love Him more than any other; this is what our relationship and our walk with God is all about.

Let's discuss the problems that are caused when level three, even though a good thing, is more powerful in our lives than level five.

When we feel called to serve in some form of mission for Jesus, we can get so in love with the people or the place we are serving that we have a hard time moving when God says it is time to go. Level three is good, but level five is what God wants for us all.

CHAPTER TWELVE

UNDERSTANDING WHY PROGRESSING THROUGH LEVELS IS ESSENTIAL FOR SERVING GOD EFFECTIVELY

Marriage - When we first consider getting married, it is rare for us to love our future spouse with level two love consistently. Eventually, we can get to the place that we love our spouse more than ourselves, but it is hard to stay at that level. If I can stay at level two and my spouse can get to level two and stay there, our marriage will be a wonderful thing to behold. Simply, I will love her more than I love me and she will love me more that she loves herself, so we both will be set on *serving* instead of *being served*. This will produce a wonderful home and a wonderful seedbed for the next generation to grown in: watching mom and dad serve each other, and serve the children as well.

Parenting - Parenting is a wonderful place to be when parents are at level two. It is rare for children to love their parents more than they love themselves, and even more rare when children love their siblings over themselves. Yet, when this is true, it is A WONDERFUL PLACE TO BE. Level two is needed for a home to be happy. When we get older and see just how much our parents had to endure to take care of us, and we are grateful, we seem to be willing to sacrifice for them as they have for us. When we become parents and realize all that our parents sacrificed for us, gratitude moves us to level two (if we were not already there). **Gratitude** is the level-changing power!

Mission motivation - When I am stuck on level one or level two, I am not going to do too much in the way of missions. I might go on a mission trip if I can take my spouse (and if it is a place where we can both can enjoy the trip), but if it requires major sacrifice, (unless we move from levels one and two to level three) we are not likely to go, even short-term. But when we are burdened for missions, we are willing to sacrifice whatever it takes to do what we know God has called us to do. Some would say that this is level five, but not really. We can go on mission trips that require some sacrifice financially, maybe even vacation time, but it is pretty safe and we are not worried about having to give our lives for Christ on this trip. If so, we are only at level three. If it is that dangerous, we simply will not be willing to go. But on the other hand, if I am at level five, it does not matter how dangerous it is; I will be willing to go. I might not take my wife, but I will be willing to go because at level five, I am willing to give whatever it takes to show love to the Master. That is the difference between level three and level five. What about level four?

Loving your enemies - Level four is loving your enemies, those whom you do not like. In the Sermon on the Mount, Jesus said to love your enemies. He said to pray for your enemies and to do good to your enemies. This is hard, but if we are getting closer to level five, I will minister to people I do not like or even people who have mistreated me without considering it too dangerous, because it is simply the right thing to do.

In Matthew 5:43-48 Jesus told His followers, *"Ye have heard that it hath been said, Thou shalt love thy neighbour, and hate thine enemy. But I say unto you, Love your enemies, bless them that curse you, do good to them that hate you, and pray for them which despitefully use you, and persecute you; That ye may be the children of your Father which is in heaven: for he maketh his sun to rise on the evil and on the good, and sendeth rain on the just and on the unjust. For if you love them which love you, what reward have ye? Do not even the publicans the same? And if ye salute your brethren only, what do ye more than others? Do not even the publicans so? Be ye therefore perfect, even as your Father which is in heaven is perfect."*

Jesus said that the rest of the world would love the people who are good to them, but His disciples will love their enemies. Simply put, if we cannot move at least to this level, we are not sure that we are truly born of God; because Jesus said, my people will be willing to do this. When you and I reach level four and we are able to get over our hurts and differences, and love our enemy, then we know that there is the presence of Jesus in us, because that simply is not normal. It is not clear that Jesus requires His people to die for Him, but He states very plainly that if you are His disciple, you will be able to love your enemy.

Remember Acts 1: 8 *"But ye shall receive power, after that the Holy Ghost is come upon you: and ye shall be witnesses unto me both in Jerusalem, and in all Judaea, and in Samaria, and unto the uttermost part of the earth."*

Did you get that? When you have the Spirit of God in you, you have level one (you will witness me), and level two (you will be a witness of me in the local Jewish areas of Jerusalem and Judea), but the next statement will require level four (Samaria and the uttermost parts of the earth). They may not have known much about the uttermost parts of the earth at this time, but they knew very well what Samaria was about, and they simply hated the Samaritans. Yet Jesus said that if they had the Holy Spirit in them, they would even share with their enemies, the people they were literally taught to hate.

Understanding martyrdom - The only way to understand a person who is willing to go to a place where they know they are more than likely be killed just because they name the name of Jesus is explained with a strong love for Jesus (level five).

And think of this verse: Luke 14:26 *"If any man come to me, and hate not his father, and mother, and wife, and children, and brethren, and sisters, yea, and his own life also, he cannot be my disciple. And whosoever doth not bear his cross, and come after me, cannot be my disciple.*

How can we even think about understanding this verse, if we do not understand level five love? The only way that we are going to be able to process this verse is to know that we must rise to the level of loving God more than anything and everything in our lives, even our own lives. This is a challenging verse, but Jesus said that if we cannot get to this level of love, we cannot be His disciple. It seems that if we are not able to love God at this level, we will not be able to understand these levels of love.

We can only hope and pray that, when and if we are asked of God to go places that are that dangerous, we will be up to that level; but remember what happened to Simon Peter. When he was asked about it, he was willing, but when it came time to do it, he was not there...interesting thought!

Overcoming strongholds - 2 Corinthians 10:4 *"(For the weapons of our warfare are not carnal, but mighty through God to the pulling down of strong holds;) Casting down imaginations, and every high thing that exalteth itself against the knowledge of God, and bringing into captivity every thought to the obedience of Christ;"*

The question is: how or why would we humans want to do what Paul told this church? We will not, unless we have moved to agape, level five love. Without settling this love issue, all other parts of our walk with God are simply out of reach.

Understanding why God asks us to tithe - We might tithe if we love ourselves, and we think if we give God 10 percent of our income, God will multiply the tithe and give us back more than we gave. This is level one tithing! Why is it level one? Simply because we would be giving to get (level one, love of self). If we hear of a mission project and we give to the mission because our heart is moved by understanding that there is such a need, this is level three love giving, but not at level five. It is important to give our offering to God out of love for Him and not love of anything or anyone else. Level five is vital to our basic service to God!

If we love God above all other of our loves, we will tithe simply because we want to please God alone. We are at level five!

Why we witness - We may witness because we love the person that we are sharing the message of salvation with, and there is nothing wrong with that; that is level two. But when we witness to a perfect stranger it is out of a love for God, as we are being obedient to him and there is nothing in it for us but to know that God is pleased. This can be level three, four or level five! However, if we had more level five love, the world would be a different place.

What is the real reason for our commitment? - You might ask yourself, "Why am I committed to God at this level or that level?" You and I must understand that everything stems from love, and where we aim our love matters. If we love ourselves alone, we serve God because there is something in it for us. If there is nothing in it for us, we simply do not serve. This is level one!

How deep are we into Jesus? - The level of our commitment answers that question! It is simply undeniable that our level of love dictates what we do not only for God but also for others.

This is my assessment as to why one is or is not willing to forsake all to follow Jesus. It is all controlled by our level of love. This is my assessment of why we do what we do and what we do not.

CHAPTER THIRTEEN

MASTERING LEVEL FIVE LOVE IS OUR ULTIMATE GOAL

- Mastering level five changes how we look at every aspect of our lives.

- Mastering level five keeps our enemy at a great distance from us.

- Mastering level five makes a good Christian a great Christian.

- Mastering level five is the sole key to Christian maturity. Level five (agape) love never fails! (1 Cor. 13)

- Mastering level five is the answer to receiving New Testament power to prevail! (Matthew 16:18)

- Mastering level five is the key to supernatural involvement with Jesus! In John chapters 14, 15 and 16 Jesus is trying to get us to understand the power with the Father when we love (agape) Jesus with level five love.

Jesus said these four things would be our life's norm if we love Him with level five love, love that moves us to surrender to His will:

1. We will experience God in ways that the rest of the world cannot even dream about!

2. We will be heard by God in ways that even other Christians can only dream about!

3. We will have the ear of God for our prayer life like never before possible.

4. We will be able to do things with the blessings of God that even Jesus Himself did not do when He was here.

Simply, Jesus said, "If you agape me …" in these chapters.

When reading John 14, 15 and 16 we notice one major thing, Jesus was telling His disciples that only a few people would be His true friends. If they agape Him, they are His friends and His friends get much from the Father. It all hinges on the agape issue here.

All these things are the blessings that come from living a life at level five love!

We can be born again and be saved, we can be baptized, we can worship God and even be at level four; but unless we are at level five, we miss the closeness of becoming a friend of Jesus.

CHAPTER FOURTEEN

BIBLICAL EXAMPLES IN LIGHT OF FIVE-LEVEL UNDERSTANDING

Adam and Eve

We have already mentioned Adam and Eve, but I did not want to look at Bible characters and leave this story out of this section.

Notice that Satan had to attack the gratitude of Adam and Eve. He attacked the issue of appreciating what God had done. He questioned what God had done for them. He questioned God's motives, and in doing so, he attacked their gratitude towards God.

Right out of the gate God began to parade this principle before us. He created this wonderful world and He gave it to a man and a woman to live in and tend. When the angels looked into the Garden of Eden, I am sure there was no way they would have thought that Adam and Eve would do what they did. The question for the ages is: why; why did they do what they did? When you understand the five love level principles, you can easily understand the failures of the two that had it all. Once the serpent suggested that Eve could have more for herself than she was getting, and she began to contemplate that, she fell to level one, took the fruit and messed up everything. However, I personally believe Adam took the fruit for a completely different reason. Think about it for a minute. Adam was still pure but she had been defiled, and would have to be separated from him. Adam took the fruit and "died" in order to keep from having to give her up. Adam ate the fruit because of level two love; he loved her more than he loved himself. Adam is a picture of Jesus here. Jesus became sin for us, He that knew no sin, to reconcile us to Himself.

Cain and Abel

God tells us in Genesis chapter 4 that Adam and Eve had two sons, and one of the sons killed the other. Cain and Abel had heard how their mom and dad once had face-to-face fellowship with God, and wanted to have that as well. Cain was a farmer. He went out into the fields, built an altar to God, and brought corn, wheat and barley, etc. Cain gave God an offering, a gift, of what he had labored to grow. We learn as we read the rest of the story that giving God a gift is alright, once we have a relationship to with Him. Yet giving God a gift will not *establish* a relationship with Him, and Cain's offering was all about what he had grown. Abel, his brother, also went out into the field and built an altar, but he took a lamb from the flock, sacrificed it, and laid it on the altar. In essence, God said, "Yes, that is it." God saw the picture of Christ in the Lamb that was slain to right the relationship between Abel and God. This created anger in the life of Cain, and as you know, Cain rose up and killed his brother. Why would Cain do such a thing? Cain fell into the zone of level one love, all he cared about at the time was how he was rejected, and Abel was accepted. Cain did not have level two love. If he had, he would have loved his brother and would have been happy for him. Cain was not far along in his relationship with God to have level five. He was stuck at level one and therefore, he killed his brother and cursed his whole legacy. Note: all the children of Cain died in the flood of Noah. Cain demonstrated jealousy, and jealousy is all about level one.

Noah

That takes us to Noah. Noah loved his family and they loved him. If this was not the case, they could not have worked in the way that they did to save their future and the human race. I do not know if they loved God at level five, seeing their relationship may not have been that far along, but we know very little about that time. We do know that they loved themselves (level one), they loved their family (level two), and Noah was a preacher for 100 years to people who were not supportive, so he must have had some level four. God used that love to motivate them to work side- by-side for over a hundred years to save the eight who rode on the Ark.

Abraham

Then we come to Abraham. Here is where God began to build a relationship with man that has progressed to the point that Abraham is motivated to show level five love. Abraham, to me, is the first one God asked to display level five love. God asked Abraham to take his son up to the top of the mountain and sacrifice him to God to display that he loved Him more than he loved his own son. As you know, this is level five.

Joseph

Joseph is Abraham's great grandson, and he (above all of Abraham's great grandsons) displayed the level four love that Abraham had. Joseph, no matter what happened to him, seemed to love God above every other person in his life. When he was with his father as a boy, you would have thought that Joseph loved his father more than anything else, but God called on him to prove his love for God over all. Joseph displayed a great deal of level five love, especially when asked to sleep with Potiphar's wife. He told her that he would not do that to his God. Level five love is clear here.

Jacob

Jacob, on the other hand, displayed a loved for himself over anyone or anything until he got to Rachel. When he saw her, he was willing to work 14 years just to have her for his wife. Jacob loved Rachel, displaying level two love, but we never see Jacob display any other love but levels one and two.

Moses

Moses, in the early years, seemed to love himself at level one, but began to show some signs of levels two and three as he killed an Egyptian to save a man (as far as we know, one that he did not even know). Level three became his focus as he turned his back on everything to finish his call to get the people of God to Canaan land. Yet later, Moses grew to display a lot of level five love for God, as nothing seemed to matter to him but pleasing God.

Samson

Samson was one of the Judges in the book of Judges. In his story we see a very self-centered, spoiled young man who wanted what he wanted and did not care whom he hurt to get it. When he wanted to get married, he told his father to get him the Philistine woman. His parents were trying to convince him to find a Jewish wife instead. Samson did not come to level four at all, unless he found it in the end. He gave his life to do what God had called him to do all along, so there is a possibility he reached level five in the end.

King Saul

King Saul never did display much over level one love. King Saul was jealous of David because of level one love, even giving his daughter to David to try to trip him up and cause him problems. Saul never reached level two that we can see, unless you consider his desire for Jonathan his son to be the next King of Israel level two love.

King David

David was a declared level five lover of God. That is why David was such a wonderful hymn writer. David wrote scores of songs, prayers, and poetry. David was the man that God said was after His own heart. David was at level five most of his life. Yet David fell back to level one. When he decided to stay home from fighting with his army, he was lying around the house and, in his boredom, fell to level one. In one afternoon, he put his own desires above his family, his kingdom, his mission, his purpose for life and even God Himself. David fell to level one, and fell hard! When he received the wages of level one sin, many endured them with him. Keep in mind that we affect many other people in the world; our love levels and their fruits affect lots of people in our lives. The life of David declares that in very powerful ways, both good and bad.

Solomon

Reading of the life of Solomon is like reading about two very different men. When he began to rule, God asked Solomon what he wanted from Him. Solomon only asked for wisdom to do what God had called him to do; God said that because he did not selfishly ask for wealth and fame, he was going to get it as a gift. However, that wealth and that fame might have contributed to his destruction. Solomon wrote the book of Proverbs and the Song of Solomon, and both of these books are wonderfully full of wisdom and blessings. When reading either of these two books, you see this wise king that loved God with all of his heart. In his older years, however, level one love came back; he simply lost his first love and became deeply miserable. When reading Ecclesiastes, which he also wrote, you can read his misery in life. This is a great lesson for us all. Even if you get all you want out of life on this side of heaven, the bottom is only a few love levels away. It is clear in reading the three books he wrote that when writing the first two he was at level five, but by the third book, he was at level one in a big way.

Solomon displayed level three when he asked for wisdom to do the mission, level two when he wrote the Song of Solomon and declared his great love for his wife, level five as he worshipped and built God's house, and level one when he wrote the book of Ecclesiastes. In a way Solomon seemed to progress in reverse: level three, then levels two, five, and then one.

Ruth

Ruth has become one of the prime examples of level two love. She became a part of her mother-in-law's world and then refused to leave her. Some say that she felt close to God when she was with Naomi; we are not sure about that. We do know that she loved Naomi enough to give up everything to follow her. She displays level two for sure.

Job

Job was a man who did everything in his power to keep his children right with God. We do not know a lot about the person of Job, but one thing we do know: Job loved his family. Job was working hard to show God that he was willing to do anything to get God to protect his children, but God required something else of Job. God required that Job love him more than anything else, even his family. God required level five love of Job and the devil came before God to test that love. No question: Job loved God at level five, which is really the message of the story of Job.

We could talk about Daniel, Elijah, Isaiah and the many prophets, especially those who gave their lives following God's calling, but whenever we find those willing to suffer for God, it is a product of level five love.

Mary, Jesus' mother

Mary, being a very young girl, exercised level five love when she was commissioned to carry the Christ child, seeing the Christ child had to be virgin born. She knew when the angel told her what God was going to do in her body that it would run head long into trouble with all who knew and loved her. However, even knowing what this news would do to her reputation and how her parents, her husband to be, her community and so on, would receive it she said, *"Be it unto me according to thy word."* (Luke 1:38). That's level five love all the way! Even as Jesus was dying for the sins of the world, she spoke not a word. Mary demonstrates a wonderful quality of level five love, faith and trust!

Joseph, Jesus' earthly father

Joseph, when approached by the angel, surrendered to the will of God and never looked back (at least, as far as we can tell). Joseph had a lot on the line as well. God was calling on Joseph to love Him enough not to question his wife; that had to be level five!

We have already discussed Simon Peter and Judas Iscariot pretty thoroughly, but most of the rest of the disciples went into level one after Gethsemane, and ran to save their own lives because of level one. All ran except one man and a few women who maintained level five through it all, loving Jesus more that their own lives.

The angel at the empty tomb had told Mary Magdalene to tell the disciples that Jesus would meet them in Galilee, but we see in John 21 that Peter and six other disciples had gone out on the Sea of Galilee fishing all night. I'm sure you know the story, as Jesus confronted them and called them to a meal on the bank. He confronted Simon about his denial by asking Simon at what level he loved Him (John 21:15-17). In essence He asked, "Do you agape (sacrificial love) Me more than these? Do you agape Me?" And then finally, "Do you phileo (brotherly love) Me? It was clear that Jesus believed that love comes in levels. He was trying to get Simon to recognize that, if he was going to be of use to Him, he would need to love Jesus at level five (agape) -- sacrificial love. This was why Peter was caught up in the denial. When we move back to level one, we are back to our own personal focus. From level one to level five cane be only a minute apart, but the results are as different as daylight and dark.

John, the apostle

John is the apostle who referred to himself in his gospel as "the one whom Jesus loved." John was a very good example of a man who loved Jesus more than himself. He made no excuses and had no reservations; and it showed in where he went, how he went, with whom he went, and how he responded when he was there. It is evident that John loved Jesus at level five. The torment John experienced proved that love; as he was exiled to the Island of Patmos, instead of becoming bitter, John wrote *"The Revelation of Jesus Christ"* (Revelation 1:1).

Mary Magdalene

Mary Magdalene was committed to Jesus and never flinched on any page of the gospels. It did not matter what was happening: from walking the streets with Jesus, to following Jesus to the cross, and even visiting the tomb on Sunday morning. Without fear, Mary Magdalene displayed level five love on every page.

One word to help us understand Mary's dedication: gratitude!

Saul/Paul

Saul/Paul was one who never seemed to care about his own safety. In turn, he was willing and able to go and do all that he did without fail, no matter what happened. As he said, *"For to me to live is Christ and to die is gain."* (Philippians 1:21)

Paul was, without question, a level five believer.

Demas

Demas has forsaken me, having loved this present world... level one!

Demas was one of the helpers of the Apostle Paul. In Colossians 4:14 Paul said, "Luke, the beloved physician, and Demas, greet you." Yet in 2 Timothy 4:10, Paul wrote *"For Demas hath forsaken me, having loved this present world, and is departed unto Thessalonica..."*

This is Paul's declaration about the loss of Demas in the service of God, and that he left the work because of what equates to love level one!

I know we have mentioned the church of Ephesus, but we must think of it in this setting. We must not forget the churches of Revelation 2 and 3, especially the church of Ephesus that had left their level five love. This church was on target, with much going for it, until the congregation slipped from agape to lower level of love. Jesus said that if we as a church did not agape God, we make Him sick (Revelation 3:15-16). He is serious about this.

We have one more scripture reference to re-visit before we close out this study. We must remember

Matthew 22:34-40, where Jesus was in the street teaching and the Pharisees and the Sadducees were questioning Him.

Vs 34 *"But when the Pharisees had heard that he had put the Sadducees to silence, they were gathered together. Then one of them, which was a lawyer, asked him a question, tempting him, and saying, Master, which is the great commandment in the law? Master, which is the great commandment in the law?" Jesus said unto him, Thou shalt love* (Agapao) *thy God with all thy heart, and with all thy soul, and with all thy mind. This is the first and great Command. And the second is like unto it, Thou shalt love* (Agapao) *thy neighbor as thyself. On these two commandments hang all the law and the prophets."*

The word here is "Agapao," which is agape, but gives the emphasis on choice. This is a command. We are to make a conscious choice to agape God, (level five love) and when we do this, we fulfill all the law and the prophets.

God created and commanded it, and Jesus modeled it and made it His total focus.

CHAPTER FIFTEEN

UNDERSTANDING THE NEED TO MOVE TO LEVEL FIVE (AGAPE) AND HOW TO STAY AT LEVEL FIVE

I hope you can see the importance to the levels and the importance of being at certain levels when we are called on to do particular tasks.

We need to move up from level one. Level one is an important place to start, but we must move up. We need to move to level two to be happily married, and we must move to level three and/or four if we are going to be on mission for God, but the ultimate is to move to level five and stay there. The question is: how do we move up to the levels that we need, and especially reach level five?

When we are in love, truly in love, we will sacrifice for our mate. When we become parents, we become sacrificing parents, and this is because we move from level one to level two. We stay at the level of two, simply because we keep our spouse and our family at a level two elevation. If we drop from level two, we are back to level one, and in turn, we become self-centered. Then our family fails. This is a very big problem and you know it. This is why this study is so important. Now we know why so many families fail. One day they are so happy but another day, they are failing. This is why!

I contend that this is the way to move to level two and stay at level two. We elevate our families' qualities above our own needs in our hearts and in turn, we set them above ourselves. Hence, Happy families! We must take control of our thoughts in order to move up the levels.

How do we get to level five and stay at level five?

As we have discussed, David discovered how to get to level five. David was one who loved God, elevating God in His heart continually. He wrote letter after letter elevating God in his life, and found himself at the highest level of love, level five!

Jesus declared His love for the Father and continued to do so modeling level five and how to stay there. Therefore, we see that level five is attained by elevating God in our lives and working to keep Him in the highest place in our lives. Mastering gratitude continually is essential. Worship, praise and exaltation of God is how to move to level five and stay at level five.

We see how the opposite is true for those who fall into destruction. In Romans 1:18-32, we see that the creation of God fell into devastation by knowing God but being unthankful. They became separated, and in a state of no return because of their ungrateful lives.

Therefore, let us never lose our song, our praise and our worship!

Paul wrote two letters to the church at Corinth, trying to get them to move away from self, and serve God through Christ. Every chapter seemed to be dealing with a problem that was driven be level one love.

1 Corinthians 3:20-21 *"...The Lord knoweth the thoughts of the wise, that they are vain. Therefore let no man glory in men..."*

1 Corinthians 4:1 *"Let a man so account of us, as of the ministers of Christ, and stewards of the mysteries of God."*

2 Corinthians 10:4-5 *"(For the weapons of our warfare are not carnal, but mighty through God to the pulling down of strongholds;) Casting down imaginations, and every high thing that exalteth itself against the knowledge of God, and bringing into captivity every thought to the obedience of Christ;"*

Even our Lord Jesus was a part of the love level zones. Jesus continually stated that He did not come to do His own will, but the will of the Father. He refused to get caught up in the zone of self.

Jesus said that He had come down from the Father and was going back to the Father. He said that the devil had a problem with the Father, and He said that He would not let Himself get caught up in the same trap as the devil. The devil gives us a picture of what happens when even an angel moves from level five to level one. He rebelled in heaven and even led a rebellion of those who also fell into level one. This tells us that even the angels in heaven who live in the presence of God live in the zones of love and are controlled by these five levels.

John 8:49 "...I honour my Father...," 8:50 "...I seek not mine own glory...," 8:54 "...If I honour myself, my honour is nothing: it is my Father that honoreth me..."

John 16:16 "...I go to the Father...," 16:28 "I came forth from the Father...," 16:32 "...the Father is with me."

Notice, it was all about the Father. The Father's will, the Father's will, the Father's will!

If we are able to do God's business, we must be all about the Father, and pull down anything that exalts itself above the Father and His glorious will!

John records the words of Jesus as they walked to the Garden of Gethsemane in John 14:15 "If ye love (agape) me, keep my commandments.", and John 14:23 "...if a man love (agape) me, he will keep my words..."

1 John 5:1-3 says, *"Whosoever believeth that Jesus is the Christ is born of God: and every one that loveth him that begat loveth him also that is begotten of him. By this we know that we love the children of God, when we love God and keep his commandments. For this is the love* (agape) *of God, that we keep his commandments: and his commandments are not grievous."*

Yes, Jesus linked together agape love for God and the keeping of the instructions of God! Therefore, we can see that Jesus declared (and the apostle John believed) that the evidence that we have passed from death unto life is if we love God enough to obey His words.

John also stated that it is a definite sign that we have become a child of God when we can love *with the love of God* -- to love God with agape love and also to love others with agape love.

1 John 4:7, 8, 9, 10, 20 and 21 make this clear: *"Beloved, let us love one another: for love is of God; and everyone that loveth is born of God, and knoweth God."* (Vs 8) *"He that loveth not knoweth not God; for God is love."* (Vs. 9) *"In this was manifested the love of God toward us, because that God sent his only begotten Son into the world, that we might live through him."* (Vs. 10) *"Here in is love, not that we love God, but that he loved us, and sent his Son..."* (Vs 20) *"If a man say, I love God, and hateth his brother, he is a*

liar: for he that loveth not his brother whom he hath seen, how can he love God whom he hath not seen?" (Vs 21) *"And this commandment have we from him, That he who loveth God love his brother also."*

It's sad to say, but there are many today who say they are Christians, believers, but are they really? Is it enough just to say that you believe Jesus was who He said He was, and did what He said He did? Is it enough just to believe, or is there more in addition to what we believe?

John believed that when we are born of God we are born of the Spirit of God, and with that Spirit comes a transformation that would manifest itself in a love (agape) for God that would move us to obey God and also to love (agape) others. This is the way to know that we are born again. When we are born again, we grow to move to levels two, three, four and five. This is the way to know that we are truly born again.

True conversion is agape love – consistent agape love! How can we expect to serve God in any effective way without growing to agape love, level five?

My prayer is that we all come to realize what declares us as Children of God and what changes us into vessels of ministry. It is agape love for sure. Remember the words of Paul in 1 Corinthians 13 :4-8 *Charity* (agape) *suffereth long, and is kind; charity* (agape) *envieth not; charity* (agape) *vaunteth not itself, is not puffed up. Doth not behave itself unseemly, seeketh not her own, is not easily provoked, thinketh no evil; Rejoiceth not in iniquity, but rejoiceth in the truth; Beareth all things, believeth all things, hopeth all things, endureth all things.* **Charity (agape) *never faileth:...*"**

I pray now we can understand this word!

CHAPTER SIXTEEN

WITH WHAT WE KNOW NOW, LET'S EXAMINE A FEW ISSUES

DANGER, DANGER, DANGER

What tools does Satan use, and what is his objective? It is important to point out that our enemy does not need to discredit God. He does not need to convince us that God is not real, or that God's word is not true. He is happy when people go down that road, but all he needs to do is to get believers to stay in level one or to move back to level one. Level one is all about me; if I am focused on me, I will easily be tricked into bringing division and destruction. When I am in a mindset to take care of me, I will be easily tripped into destruction. Let me give a few examples of this:

<u>Offense</u>—Jesus made it clear that it would be a problem when one gets offended. He told John the Baptist not to get offended in Matthew 11:6 *"...blessed is he, whosoever is not offended in me."* John was about to be killed and Jesus was not going to rescue him, so Jesus encouraged him not to get caught up in being offended on his way to die. Offense causes us to get in the "I" zone; and being in that place is not

healthy for a servant of God, even when you are John the Baptist.

Jesus told His disciples that they would become the enemies of the Jewish people, and they would be hated because they were a part of His world. He told them this to prevent them from being offended at Him.

It is important that we do not become offended at God, but He also told us not to be offended at our brothers, either. In Matthew 18, Jesus spent a great deal of time explaining the importance of staying away from being offended at our brothers and sisters. Jesus knew that offense is a hammer that Satan uses to divide and conquer. The reason this tool is so effective for our enemy is because, when we are offended, we run back to level one; and in level one we are in a position of sin.

We must stay out of the vacuum of self! We must say to ourselves, "NO SELF, NO SELF, NO SELF!" Offense is a trap! Do not get caught in the trap of offense!

Affiliation—We also must be careful about with whom we affiliate. Our enemy also wants us to get friendly with people who are not good for us (nor our new life in Christ). The goal of bad friends and relations is always to take us back to level one; and in level one we make many mistakes that we would not make if we are in any number other than level one.

We must be careful not to allow our life in Christ to be affiliated with those who would take us back to level one. It is an important test for our relationships. If the person or persons are pushing us to level five, we can consider them a good circle of friends. If not, run!

Sin—Sin is a word that is produced when we suffer from self-worship. Self-worship is from level one. When one commits sin, it is because one either never left level one or has moved back to level one.

Romans 6:12-13 *"Let not sin therefore reign in your mortal body, that ye should obey it in the lusts thereof. Neither yield ye your members as instruments of unrighteousness unto sin: but yield yourselves unto God..."*

When sin reigns, we are servants to it, and we are in level one. It is "all about me" when sin reigns. Think about any sin that is causing problems in people's lives; the sin would have no power without level one. Level one is the danger zone. Again, when we are in level one, we are in the "I" zone.

The answer is to yield yourself unto God. Get out of level one and to level five as fast as you can. NO SELF, NO SELF, NO SELF!

With this knowledge, read this verse with new eyes, level one, eyes. Col. 3:5 *"Mortify therefore your members which are upon the earth; fornication (sex outside of God's design), uncleanness, inordinate affection, evil concupiscence (earthly desires), and covetousness, which is idolatry:"* (Vs. 8) *"...put off all these; anger, wrath, malice, blasphemy, filthy communication out of your mouth."*

No question - God wants us to move from the sin zone, but how do we put these things away? We do so by staying away from level one. All these are products of level one.

I hope you can see that level one is not a place where God-fearing believers want to live. Every sinful and destructive act on the planet needs level one to exist. Just as you need oxygen, fuel and friction to make a fire, sin needs level one to create an atmosphere for sin to thrive.

Adultery, pornography addiction, divorce, gambling, cheating, fighting, pride, homosexuality, abortion, drug addiction, lying, etc., all have one thing in common for these things to be part of our lives: level one.

What is the answer to level one?

Jesus put it this way:

- Surrender your life to Christ and **repent** of your sinful self, turn from level one!

- Surrender yourself to serve, and do so by declaring yourself ministering agents of God by baptism. **Baptism** is a declaration of turning from level one to serve God. Read Romans 6:3 *"Know ye not, that so many of us as were baptized into Jesus Christ were baptized into His death?"*

- Read the Sermon of Jesus in Matthew 5-7, and see how **surrendering to service** and staying away from self empowers us. "Blessed are the poor in spirit," "Blessed are they that mourn," "Blessed are the meek," "Blessed are they which do hunger and thirst after righteousness," "Blessed are the merciful," "Blessed are the pure in heart," "Blessed are the peacemakers," "Blessed are they which are persecuted for righteousness' sake," "Blessed are ye, when men shall revile you, and persecute you," "Rejoice and be exceeding glad: for great is your reward in heaven." Notice: none of these statements could be experienced if we are living in level one.

- **Serve others**! Jesus showed His disciples how to serve by washing His disciples' feet in John 13 as a display of servanthood, and He told His disciples to go and serve others as well.

- **Communion**—Jesus gave us a picture of what it means to be in communion with God and with man. Jesus was willing to die to self in order to produce the kingdom in us. In taking part in the communion of Christ, we too are entering into a mode of self-denial in order to serve alongside Christ.

- **Commission**—Jesus gave us a job to do that would take great sacrifice in order to be obedient to it. (Mark 16:15) *"...Go ye into all the world and preach the gospel to every creature."* This is an action that will not be realized in level one. None who try to be a part of this commission will ever do so without moving from level one. We must move up the love levels in order to fulfill this commission.

Less of me and more of Him. Less of me and more of my family. Less of me and more of the commission. Less of me and more of love for my enemies, the Samaritans. Less of me and more of God!

Our weapon—God has called us to stay away from level one, self-love, but what power motivates us outside of these callings? How do we do this? What is the power that moves us from level one? **One word—gratitude!**

Paul told the Romans that they were in great trouble because they were not thankful in Romans 1:21 *"...when they knew God, they glorified Him not as God, neither were thankful; but became vain in their imaginations, and their foolish heart was darkened."* **Level one!**

Gratitude is the key to moving from level one to level five. Gratitude is the key word that will motivate us to stay away from level one and serve others. Level one is not a good place to live. When you are experiencing troubles, look for level one and (more times than not) you will see it! Experiencing good: more times than not, you will see any level but level one.

CHAPTER SEVENTEEN

A PERSONAL NOTE

It is so vital that we Christians understand the levels, and where we are in relation to this love scale. If we are married with a family, we must move to level two or we will not have a good marriage. It is so important when we understand these things that we do not settle for anything less than level five in our personal lives. God has given His only begotten Son not only to redeem us and to pay our grave sin debt, reconciling us to Himself, but He has called us to love in a big way, a level five way. He modeled that level five love on the cross.

Eph. 2:15-18 *"Having abolished in His flesh the enmity, even the law of commandments contained on ordinances; for to make in himself of twain one new man, so making peace; And that he might reconcile both unto God in one body by the cross, having slain the enmity thereby: And came and preached peace to you which were afar off, and to them that were nigh. For through him we both have access by one Spirit unto the Father."*

Col. 1:20-22 *"And, having made peace through the blood of his cross, by him to reconcile all things unto himself; by him, I say, whether they be things in earth* or things in heaven. And you, that were sometime alienated and enemies in your mind by wicked works, yet now hath he reconciled In the body of his flesh through death, to present you holy and unblamable and unreprovable in his sight:"

2 Cor. 5:18 "And all things are of God, who hath reconciled us to himself by Jesus Christ, and hath given to us the ministry of reconciliation;"

This was not just to take us to heaven when we die, but to model to the world what level five love looks like and to empower us to be able to live like no others on the planet.

Jesus said that He was going to build a church (ecclesia) group of called out ones that would be so empowered that Satan and all of death and hell would be powerless. **How can these things be?** After learning these things, it becomes clear that Jesus' intent for His disciples is this type of power. When we read His words, it is clear that this type of power would only come when His followers love Him consistently at level five. The gates of hell are crippled and the gates of heaven are at our beckon call when level five is our life. **Why would you say that?** In Matthew 16, Jesus named Simon Peter, he also said that he would be able to ask for things in heaven and get it, *"whatsoever thou shalt bind on earth shall be bound in heaven: and* *whatsoever thou shalt loose on earth shall be loosed in heaven."* **That is something special!**

When we understand all five levels, it is important to be able to live all of them well, but the supernatural power is really in level five. When we reach level five, it is amazing. As Paul said, **"Agape never fails." Level five never fails! Notice in Matt. 16:23, where Jesus called Simon Peter "Satan." Why did this happen? This is a perfect example of how we can shift from 1 to 5 and 5 to 1 in just a few minutes.**

It is apparent that love is the motivating factor of every aspect of our lives. Remember, when Jesus was asked what is the greatest commandment, He said *"Thou shalt love (agape) the Lord thy God with all thy heart, and with all thy soul, and with all thy mind. This is the first and great commandment. And the second is like unto it, Thou shalt love (agape) thy neighbour as thyself. On these two commandments hang all the law and the prophets."* He went on to say that if you could conquer this, you could conquer all. Remember that the words here in Jesus' statement demonstrate agape -- level five.

I just want us to know that Jesus constantly pushed level five as the key to success in every area.

Love motivates us because we love ourselves, which is basic, but if we do not have a healthy love for ourselves, we will have other problems. Why? Because everything, every decision, affects the provision for oneself. We do everything for personal gain or the fear of personal loss. Even our relationship with God is created and motivated with this in mind. If we want to go to heaven, we accept the payment made by Jesus for our sins. If we do not want to be rejected and sent to hell, the place of pain and torment, described in Luke 16:22-31, we accept the payment made by Jesus for our sins. Therefore, even our personal salvation is motivated by the love of self, which moves us to reach for personal gain and to retreat from personal loss. God has created in humans this desire and this fear, and if these two are missing, the person is in trouble from the beginning. Therefore, God encourages healthy self-love. But if self-love stays, and that is the only love we have, we become a very selfish and miserable person. We make everyone in our world miserable as well, because we are so focused on selfish gain. But if we grow to level two, we become a blessing to the other people in our world.

John told us that God is love! God is level five! Jesus wants us to grow and progress to level five. This is what Jesus was saying Luke 14, when He told the story of a certain man who made a great supper and invited many to the meal. When He called certain ones to come to the meal, they began to make excuses. One said he had bought a field and he had to go see it.

Another said that he had purchased a yoke of oxen and needed to go and prove them; another said that he had taken a wife. All had excuses, and it was apparent that even though he had labored to provide a meal for his friends, they did not think enough of him to come and eat with him. They had other things that were more important that they needed to take care off. Then He said, in verse 26 *"If any man come to me, and hate not his father, and mother, and wife and children, and brethren, and sisters, yea, and his own life also, he cannot be my disciple."*

Why is this such a big issue? To be Jesus' disciple is to go where Jesus says to go and do what Jesus says to do, even if you may have to die to do it. This takes level five love; if we do not have level five, we will not be able to be His disciples. This gives us an understanding as to why some are willing to give their lives. Level five!

You might ask, "Why did you go back to this verse?" Because I want you to see its context. Jesus gave a level five declaration because level one will not do if we are going to be His disciple. Levels one, two, three and four will not do. Level five is what is needed to be able to be a true disciple.

God wanted us to know that He loved His creation more than He loved His own son. He demonstrated that love by the sacrifice on the cross. If we confess our sinfulness, accept and embrace the Christ who gave Himself for us, trust Him for our eternity, and ask God to take the death of His Son and apply it to our accounts, we will be saved. As I know I am a product of God's love for me, I now am trying to grow in love for God and His son, to be able to *live* for Christ as well as die for him. When we grow in grace as Peter tells us to do, we are really growing in our levels of love, moving from level one up to level five and trying to stay there. This is where Jesus wanted Simon Peter as they sat by the Sea of Galilee, and He asked him, "Do you love me more than these?" He asked, however, "Do you agape Me?" He was asking Simon for agape, level five love. Simon had always tried to be in the level five zone. He had claimed that he was there a few times, but this time, he would not say that he loved Jesus with the agape love. He knew that he had claimed to have that love before, but did not have enough for the trial he faced at the time. Nevertheless, from what we have read, Simon Peter actually did grow to the level five zone, and was willing to give his life for Jesus, so tradition tells us.

The question is: on what level of love are you today, and how do you get to level five with God (and stay there)?

Let us just look at a few of God's biblical stories, see how these principles will help us understand God's desire for our lives and how understanding and applying them will bless you, your family, and others areas of your life. In light of what we now know, we can see the love levels in every story and on every page. We see why people do what people do.

CHAPTER EIGHTEEN
CONCLUSION

We have examined many actions and many life choices, and how those choices change the direction of our lives. Individual choices made at certain moments have the potential of blessing and cursing our future and the future of those who follow us. They change the direction of individuals, families and even nations. In the example in Genesis Chapter 9, we see that the son of Noah, Ham, had his son with him as he visited his father when Noah lay naked in his tent. We do not know what happened there, but we do know that God says that, because of a decision there in that tent, Ham's son, Canaan, was sentenced to serve his brother (Gen. 9:27 *"God shall enlarge Japheth, and he shall dwell in the tents of Shem; and Canaan shall be his servant."* Some have asked why God took the land from Canaan and gave it to the Israelites in Joshua chapter 1 and here we find that it was all because of a decision that was made there. Specifically, what that decision was is not mentioned, but it cost Canaan his land and the land of his ancestors. That is the power of this material! If we understand these things, it will change our lives. This understanding needs to be shared. Love of self, love of others over self, love of missions (people we do not know), love for our enemies, and last but certainly not least, love for God. This information has the ability to change the world! I pray that it at least changes you and me.

We have discovered and declared the power behind decisions, the levels of love that influence us at the moment of decision. When we see this powerful force and just how powerful it is, we can look back in time and see why people made the decisions they did. After understanding these levels, we can understand why we have marriage, divorce, commitment and non-commitment, faithful servanthood and faithless servants, and destructive behavior and why it exists. It is all powered by love and which level the person is in at the time of the decision!

God told Moses in Leviticus 17:11 *"For the life of the flesh is in the blood..."* In the world of medicine, one of the greatest advances was when we finally discovered ways to measure the blood, test the blood and discover what is missing and what is present in the blood that should not be there. This knowledge allowed new diagnoses in many situations, and the world of medicine has never been the same. I believe that this, too, has the potential of transforming the biblical community, the counseling community, and every other area of life, especially marriage and relationships.

My hope is that we can take this information and walk filled with love at the right level. Maybe, with this knowledge, we can conduct our lives in a way that produces a great future, blessing our children and our children's children. Maybe we can reach level five, and in so doing, redirect our hearts to produce a love for God that will bless Him.

Notice, when Jesus was asked, which commandment was the greatest (Matthew 22), He did not hesitate. He paraphrased Deuteronomy 6:5 *"...thou shalt love the LORD thy God with all thine heart, and with all thy soul, and with all thy might."* He then added to it, *"...love thy neighbour as thyself...,"* (Matthew 22:39). Do these two things, and you will have taken care of the whole law. He said, love God at level five and love others above level one, and you will be in good standing with God.

Knowledge is power, and when we put this knowledge to work in our lives, we will be in harmony with Jesus. You just cannot get any better than that on this side of glory or, may I say, on the other side.

That says it all. I believe we must understand these levels and the need to make a choice to move to level five and stay there. This is the will of God in Christ Jesus, and the success or failure of life hangs on our ability to do this.

May God Bless you in your quest to become a level five follower of God through the Savior Jesus Christ.

CHAPTER NINETEEN
A BONUS, BUT A MUST

I want to take a moment and make sure that anyone who reads this material understands that Jesus desires to save him or her. It is important that we all come to Jesus, ask for forgiveness, and enter into a relationship with Him through repenting and believing. We came to be in rebellion when Adam and Eve, our spiritual parents, acted out in levels one and two, and we return back to God by moving from level one to repentance, turn to God with a simple request for forgiveness, and surrender.

"I pray that when you have finished reading these thoughts you are much wiser as to how the human heart works, and why it is important to elevate others (especially God) above yourselves. This is healthy. I also pray that you are a reader who has trusted Jesus to forgive your sins and bring you into relationship with Him. If not, I ask you to pray this prayer to God. "Heavenly Father I know that I am a sinner and am in desperate need of a Savior. I ask you to forgive me of my sin debt and bring me into relationship with You. Let me grow to love You, Lord Jesus, more than myself, and even more than everyone and everything in my life. I give myself to you and surrender to your wonderful will for my life. In the powerful name of Jesus I pray, Amen!"

Now you have done what Romans 10:13 says: *"For whosoever shall call upon the name of the Lord shall be saved."*

Now I encourage you to find yourself a body of believers, a church in your area that preaches the whole word of God and exalts Jesus. Please do me the honor of sending me an email letting me know what God is doing in your life, if this book has been of help to you. Send your message to <u>Info@Pvbchurch.com</u>. I look forward to hearing from you. God Bless you in your search for joy in a world of level one.

God's Love Codes Questions:

Introduction:

1. What is the most powerful force in heaven or on earth? Discuss the reason for your answer.
2. Discuss why you think Satan and a third part of the angels turned away from God.

Ch. 1:

1. Why do you think April and Julie responded so differently when faced with the same questions, even though their life experiences were so similar?
2. Why did Ben stay true to his wife even though many others would have strayed?
3. Why would a young women named Asia Bibi be willing to sacrifice so much for her faith?
4. Read 2nd Samuel 11 and discuss why David, the man after God's own heart, would do what he did even though he knew that it was going against God's will for him.
5. In light of these four examples, discuss why you think people do what they do even though they know that it is wrong.

Ch. 2:

1. In light of God's 10 Commandments, discuss why Jesus, when asked which command is the greatest, said we are to love God and our neighbors.
2. When Jesus confronted Simon Peter in John 21, why was this conversation all about love?
3. Discuss the difference in the words used for love in this chapter and why that is such an important issue.

Ch. 3:

1. It seems clear that all of our relationships are dependent on love. Discuss why understanding the different words used for love is important to us as we understand each other.
2. In John 3:16, which word for love was used by Jesus, and why is this word so important in this passage?
3. When Abraham was directed to take his son up the mountain and sacrifice him, what is this story saying about what kind of love is needed to be God's man?
4. Explain how the story of Abraham was continued in John 3.

5. What are the two Greek words for love used in John 21, and why are they so important?

Ch. 4:

1. Biblical levels of love were explained in John 21. Discuss other pictures of love levels in the Bible discussed by the author.
2. What other examples can you name that highlight the different levels shown in the biblical stories?
3. Can you name a few modern examples of these levels? Take a few minutes and see how many examples you can name.
4. In 1st Corinthian 13, Paul said, "Love never fails." Which love was he talking about?
5. In Revelation 2:4, what did the author of Revelation mean when he said, "Thou hast left thy first love?"
6. How does Revelation 2:4 demonstrate that love comes in levels?
7. How did John 21 demonstrate love levels as Jesus asked, "Do you love me more than these?"

Ch. 5:

1. Take a few minutes and explain each love level and give examples of each.

2. Why is level five what Jesus wanted from Simon Peter?
3. In light of this understanding in John 21, can you tell me why Asia Bibi was willing to go to prison instead of denying Christ, especially when she knew what would happen to her family if she stayed true to Christ?
4. In light of John 21, why were April and Julie's responses so different in the introduction?

Ch. 6:

1. Explain what happened to Eve in the Garden of Eden in light of what we now know about love levels?

Ch. 7:

1. As we see Eve go from level five to level one in the Garden of Eden, what level was Adam in when he ate the fruit, according to this author?
2. When Simon Peter promised to go to prison or death with Jesus in Luke 22, what level of love was he in at the time of promises?
3. When Simon denied Christ three times, what level was he in then?
4. What was the event that caused Simon to move from level five to level one?

5. Does this mean that we can change levels throughout our day?
6. What word did this writer say caused Simon Peter to deny and Judas to betray?
7. In Luke 22, Jesus told Simon Peter to strengthen the brethren, what level of love was Jesus pushing him to?
8. Beware of offense! Why did this author say this? What does offense cause us to do?

Ch. 8:

1. What did this author say was the level we need to stay away from after salvation?
2. What level is the one that declares that we are spiritualty mature?
3. When Paul said in 1ˢᵗ Corinthian 13 that he once was a child but needed to move to manhood, what level is maturity?

Ch. 9:

1. Explain David's life of love and failure in light of what you now know about the five levels.
2. As the Apostle Paul said in 2ⁿᵈ Corinthians 5:14, "For the love of Christ constrains us," what does that mean in light of what you now know about these levels?

3. When reading Paul's letter to the Corinthian Church, Paul explained why he loved Christ. What was the reason?
4. John also wrote in 1 John 4:19 "We love (agape) Him, because He first loved (agape) us. Discuss this statement in light of what you now know.
5. In Romans Chapter 1, what does our love for God say about what will happen in our future?
6. When Jesus declared the coming of persecution in John 15, what kind of love was He telling the disciples that they would need?

Ch. 10:

1. Discuss the extreme importance of understanding moving from level one to any other level, and how it affects what we do or do not do.

Ch. 11:

1. Discuss why it is so important for us to understand and to think in levels as we make decisions.
2. What do you think would have happened in Abraham's life if he had loved his mother and father more than God when he was told to leave Ur in Genesis 12?

Ch. 12:

1. How does understanding these five levels help us in our marriage?
2. How does understanding these levels help us in our parenting?
3. Discuss how we will not fulfill the Great Commission given to us in Matthew 28: 18- if we do not move to level five?
4. Discuss how our understanding of level five helps us understand martyrdom?
5. How does understanding these levels help us understand why God asked us to tithe and give a portion of our income?

Ch. 13:

1. Discuss why the goal of every Christian should be to master level five.
2. In John 14, 15, 16, Jesus said that His friends would be those who love (agape) Him. Explain this principle.
3. In light of what we see in these levels, can a born again believer be saved and live in any other level but level five?

Ch. 14:

1. In reading chapter fourteen, look at each of these biblical characters and explain their success and failures based on the five levels.

Ch. 15:

1. As Paul wrote to the Church at Corinth, what was he trying to move them away from? Explain your answer.

Ch. 16:

1. When reading this material, what is one word that we must stay away from in order to love God at level five?
2. In Matthew 11:6, why was it so important that John the Baptist refuse to be offended at Jesus, even when he did not understand the circumstances?
3. When one sees the word sin, what level is at the center of this word?
4. When reading Luke 14:26 "If any man come to me, and hate not his father, and mother, and wife and children, and brethren, and sister, yea, and his own life also, he cannot be my disciple." what is He saying in light of what you now know?

Conclusion:

Discuss how understanding these love level principles will change your life.

What is the most important thing that you learned in this study?

Now I will ask you the same question that was asked in the introduction: What is the most powerful force in Heaven and or on earth?

And I will also ask again: In light of what we have discussed, why do people do what they do?